Stop

STORIES & POEMS ABOUT DOMESTIC VIOLENCE AND SEXUAL ABUSE

By Colleen Williams

P.O. Box 402
Swiftwater, PA 18370
(973) 348-5067
sspublishingcompany@gmail.com

www.sharsheypublishingcompany.com

Copyright © **2020 Colleen Williams**
ISBN- 13: **978-1-7348030-0-6**
Publisher: S*har- Shey Publishing Company LLC*
Book Cover Designed by: *Dynasty's Visionary Designs*
Typesetting: *LaQueisha Malone*

Edited by: *ATW Editing*

All rights reserved. No part of this book may be reproduced or transmitted in any form or by any means, electronic or mechanical, including photocopying, recording, or by any information storage and retrieval system, without permission in writing from the copyright owner. This book was printed in the United States of America.

TABLE OF CONTENTS

5	Introduction
7	Forgiveness
12	She Wasn't Supposed to be Here
18	She Kept Ignoring the Red Flags
47	Why
48	I Get It
50	I Was That Woman
54	I Sit and Wait
57	I Will Be Your Voice
60	A Letter To My Abusive Exes
66	Above It All, It Ends Today
93	I Do
103	As I Leave You
112	A Message to the Ladies
115	A Letter to the Ladies
119	But I Love Him
123	I Love /Hate You (pick one)
125	It Happened Again
129	When Will It End?
131	She Is No Longer Here
133	I Dance, I Rise, I Demand
135	Here I Stand
136	No Longer Black and Blue
139	In Memory Of...
142	Did You Hear About?
145	Don't Stay, You Run Away
148	Too Broken to be Fixed
151	Men Are Victims Too
153	My Little Secret
175	Sexual Abused

176	Being Sexually Abused
178	Behind the Windows of My Soul
182	He Said She Said
184	My Life Matters, So I Spoke Up
186	He Touched Me
189	A Letter to the Man Who Molested Me
197	Taking Back My Power
199	I Survived
201	You Are Not Alone and It Wasn't Your Fault
205	A Prayer
206	Acknowledgments
212	About the Author

INTRODUCTION

To every woman who had to apologize to their children for what they had to go through. I'm sorry.

To every woman who had to send their children outside or somewhere else so they can't see or hear the abuse. I'm sorry.

To every woman who had to flinch at every little thing that triggered them. I'm sorry.

To every woman who had to explain to someone else what happened or had to lie or make an excuse for your pain, your battered and bruised body. I'm sorry.

To every woman who thought it was their fault. It wasn't.

To every woman who took the blame, you didn't have to lie for him to protect him.

To every woman that died. Rest in peace.

For every woman I lost to domestic violence. I'm sorry I couldn't help.

To every man that had to deal with a broken woman or had to heal her broken heart or had to fix what another man has broken or had to sit up all night to hear about her hurtful past. I thank you.

For every woman that is reading this. If you are in a domestic violence relationship, GET OUT NOW.

FORGIVENESS

We must start with forgiveness. Forgiveness equals healing and healing equals peace. In order for me to write this book, I had to completely forgive all my abusers. As I sit here at the park sipping on my green tea, watching the birds fight for a piece of crust, I glance at the innocent kids playing on the swings, running behind each other, playing 'tag, you're it.' I shake my head and smile. I wish I had a life like theirs. I had a hard life growing up. I didn't have a joyous childhood. I endured more than I can handle, which caused me to have so much hatred and pain. It started with the abandonment I received from my mother when she left me in Trinidad, which was followed by sexual abuse, the lies, the betrayal, the disrespect, the hurt from my past relationships, the backstabbing friends, the cheating and abusive husband. I tried to forgive, but it was hard. I wanted to hurt them the way they hurt me, but I knew that was not the right way to handle things. I held it in for many years. I didn't know how to forgive.

Numerous times I asked God why he couldn't take me now. I didn't want to be on earth if my whole life people were going to hurt me and expect me to keep forgiving them. I thought it would have been easy, but I realized it was not easy. I forgave the people who hurt me. I talked to them. I let them know how much pain they caused me, but it stayed in my mind and my heart. I couldn't let go. I felt it wasn't enough; I wanted them to feel what I was feeling. I almost lost it when I realized I was only hurting myself. I took some time. I did some deep soul searching, spiritual cleansing, disconnected myself from a lot of people. I was ready to face the world again, but this time I knew I could not allow anyone to hurt me again; this time I set high standards. My wall went up. I knew if I didn't forgive, I would still be harboring the pain. I didn't want to carry it on to the next relationship. It would not be fair for the next person to suffer for what others did.

Forgiveness, to me, is accepting what already happened, working it out, talking about it. Once you forgive, let it go and move on.

I spent a lot of time in the hospital. I would say in one year, I was there at least 50 times, if not more. One day I was rushed to the hospital. I knew I was too young to have a heart attack; my blood pressure was fine, all the blood work came back great, I took a stress test and it was extremely high. All the nurses and doctors came in and out of the room, but this one doctor walked in the room where I was laying and gave me a piece of her mind. I knew she was tired of seeing me there. She knew I was dealing with a lot. She could see it and she felt it. As I tried to wipe my tears so she wouldn't see, she held my hand and said, "Sweetheart whatever you are holding on to, you have to forgive." I was going back and forth with her, asking her what she was talking about. She said, "Whatever it is, you have to let it go, you have to forgive those who hurt you." I was looking at her like, "Why is she telling me all this?" And of course, she saw my chart; she knew how many times I'd been there, how many times I passed out, or had anxiety attacks.

When she told me stress kills, and if I keep harboring this pain it can lead to silent stress and I can die, I came home and let it go. I went in my room and shut the door and just cried uncontrollably. I prayed to God to give me the strength to forgive so I could have peace with myself. I cried. I released it all. I felt the emptiness. I felt a weight lifted off my shoulders that I did not have to carry anymore.

I know this lady who never forgave her family for abandoning her and putting her in an orphanage. All her life she was angry and bitter; she took it out on everyone she came in contact with at home, work and even in public. Everyone felt her nasty energy. She was never able to let go. She carried this heavy, painful weight with her for over 30 years. Every time I came in contact with her, I told her she would not have anyone at her funeral because she was just bitter and angry and negative all day, every day. I tried to understand her. I gave her advice. I even shared my story, but it was not enough; she never let go. Till today, as I write this, she is still holding on to the pain. It affected and infected a lot of people. I always wondered; how can she live like that? The sad part is she lost a lot of people; they did not die, they just removed themselves from her because it was too much. She refused to let go and get help. Half of the people she is still talking about are dead and gone, so clearly, she is wasting time holding on. I knew I didn't want to turn out like her. I couldn't hold on that long to any kind of pain. I kept telling her she has to forgive; if she keeps holding on, she will not be able to see what is in front of her.

Forgiving is such an easy word, but it is one of the hardest things you can do. It's not like quitting smoking or drinking or giving up a bad habit. But when you do, it's like a heavy weight being lifted off your shoulders. I am glad I was able to forgive all my abusers so now I can help and teach others how and why it is so important to forgive. I'm not trying to get biblical, but the Bible has ample scriptures about forgiveness that can ease your pain and teach you how to forgive and why you should forgive. One of my favorites is Luke 23 verse 34.

If God can forgive us (and we sin every single day) who are we not to forgive?

What if God gave up on us? Please, by all means, I'm not saying pick up the phone and call everyone and say I forgive you. I'm just saying it's easier to forgive and move on than to harbor all that pain you are holding on to. Try it. People ask what took me so long to forgive. Half of it was way beyond my control and when you are living with the person who is hurting you it's not easy to walk away, but as you get older you get wiser. You will never know how much power an abuser has over their victim. I was able to forgive.

I shut my room door and just surrendered to God. I asked him to help me forgive all those who hurt me and let me down. I read scriptures. I had to be patient and wait.

SHE WASN'T SUPPOSED TO BE HERE

Years ago, I heard about this girl in my area that was left for dead at age seven. I overheard her mother's boyfriend was touching her in some not-so-nice places. She actually told someone. But the next day her body was found with her head busted open in a ravine. I heard she survived, thank God for that.

Another young girl from my area was sexually abused between the ages of 9 to 13 by a neighbor who was supposed to be watching her while her mother went away. She was lost and confused and couldn't get an explanation as to why she had to endure that type of abuse. But not having any family or an outlet, she had to endure years of pain and torture. She finally left the house of horrors and went to go live with her mom.

I know everybody remembered the Michael Jackson song "Beat it" and the belt with the iron spikes; just imagine her getting beaten with that belt every day for nothing. The abuse continued for years.

STOP

She finally got away and ran into her first love (her son's father). After years of abuse, she finally felt loved, but that didn't last long. She got pregnant right away. He left her six months pregnant. She became homeless, living from shelter to shelter, trying to survive.

A lot of people were still talking about her. They were so happy to hear she got away from all that abuse and met a man of God. Yesssss... I think she deserves nothing but the best! We all do. He promised her he would give her everything in the world; anything she wanted was hers. But what he didn't tell her was that it came with black eyes, broken bones, hospital visits, disrespect, cheating, lies and that one ass whipping that would land her in the ICU. He really loved her; he even worshipped the ground she walked on and promised her he would love her to death. Yup, you heard me right. LOVE HER TO DEATH. The same ground he worshipped was the same ground he threw her down on and stomped her with his construction boots... He married her, got her right where he wanted her, beat her, and kicked her in her head, stomach, and face. He also threw her on the bed and raped her while his revolver was in her mouth. She ended up getting pregnant and thought the baby would change his ways. Yeah, okay. Sadly, he kicked the baby right out of her stomach.

Yeah, I know y'all sitting there saying: *She is stupid, why didn't she call the cops?* Well, she did. They came, but he was also a police officer and when did you ever hear of an officer locking up their own partner? They had to stick together, right? I'm sure they abuse their wives at home too. Who knows?

Well, what do you know? I saw her the other day. I am so happy for her. She found love once again in the arms of another Godly man, a pastor. (You would think she had learned her lesson about these so-called men of God.)

They say a man who brings you close to God is a man to keep. Yeah, right. First of all, God is not lost, so a man can't bring you close to Him. He needed to find God find himself, then come find her. He had to know her pain. I mean, he read her books, right? They got married but he forgot to tell her he was already married. After months of verbal, mental, physical, financial, emotional and spiritual abuse, he wanted to protect her. How sweet! So, he took out an accidental life insurance policy on her. Yup, you heard me. "Accidental." You know, just in case something randomly happened to her. For her 44th birthday, he set her up to get robbed and killed. Happy Birthday to her. There was one in the chamber, but the revolver jammed. Well, if that wasn't protection from God, then I don't know what that was.

This woman was looking for love in all the wrong places; however, she never gave up. She dated guys who all ended up being abusive. She decided enough is enough. She took some time to be alone and focus on herself, learning how to get past her past. After being celibate for a whole year, she went out on a date; he ended up stealing her credit card, rang it up, and her account was overdrawn. Poor woman can't catch a break. I recently got an email from her. I was concerned about her, like how much more can she take? She picked herself back up again.

Oh, I forgot to tell you, she lost her father eight years ago from cancer. Her mother never loved her. She was called a mistake her entire life. She lost her older brother on June 14th. She lost her younger brother July 30th. Her heart stopped July 9th. She lost her niece on October 14th in a car accident; she lost her sister on April 21st due to complications of surgery. She lost 46 women to domestic violence in the past two years. You know the sad part of this whole story?

That little girl and woman I told y'all about? That was me. Yup, that's right. Me.

This woman is now the CEO of her t-shirt line STOPMOVEMENTTEES. My t-shirt inspires women to get out and stay out. I am also an author of three books. I am also a dancer, choreographer, teacher, soccer coach, model and an advocate for domestic violence and sexual abuse. I travel the world speaking to men and women in prisons, jails and shelters, teaching them how to go from bitter and broken to beautiful and blessed. I am now a wife: trust me I dotted all the I's and crossed the T's on this one.

Listen to me: I was sexually abused,
raped, left for dead.
My ex-husband set me up,
put a gun to my head.
If you noticed, I kept leaving,
I didn't stay.
I didn't let them, or anything
get in my way.
With faith, favor and grace
I tied up my laces and ran my own race.
I came from the ghetto,
didn't have a mother or a father
So, you know my life
was two times harder
Never put a question mark
where God puts a period.
Psalms chapter 139 verse 14 says
I am fearfully and wonderfully made.
Never let anyone tell you
what you can and cannot do,
when Philippians 4:13 clearly says

STOP

*I can do all things through Christ
who strengthens me.
Don't give up on God,
because he won't give up on you.
Faith without work is dead.
You can't say you have faith,
but don't work towards it.
You can't sit down and keep complaining
about your problems and expect it to change.
Where there is life there is hope.
Stop going back where you just asked
God to remove you from.
Look at what I went through;
look at where I am now.
Won't he do it?*

SHE KEPT IGNORING THE RED FLAGS

It's Saturday morning and I'm up, dragging myself out of my big queen-size bed. It's also my one-year anniversary from leaving my abusive ex-husband who held me at gunpoint for two days in my room. I'm thankful for God and my best friend Indigo for helping me get out safe. Indigo and I have been best friends since 3rd grade. We always spend the night over at each other's house. We do everything together; we go everywhere together. Some people think we are sisters. Our mothers both died in a car accident while they were on their way to watch our last soccer game before we went off to college. It was a hard hit for us both. Ever since that day we made a vow to never leave each other and we kept that from high school till now. *I miss you, Mom. I'm going to make you proud.* I'm going back to sleep and enjoy my Saturday. I hope no one disturbs me.

    My alarm has been going off for the past five minutes. I kept pressing snooze. It's Saturday morning. I just dozed right back into a deep sleep.

"Who is it?" I yelled as I answered my cell phone.

"It's me, Indigo."

"What do you want, girl? It's 6:00 in the morning. This better be an emergency."

"You promised me you would go to the gym with me."

"Oh, shoot. I forgot. I told you I would go with you one day. Okay? I'll go later. I'm going back to sleep."

"Naila, come on."

"I'll be ready in 30 minutes."

"It's not like we have to drive there. It's right across the court in the apartment complex, so get up and get dressed," she said as she hung up.

I crawled out from under the covers, looking a hot mess. I'm not a morning person, but okay. I jumped in the shower, brushed my teeth, washed my face, threw my hair in a ponytail, threw on a pair of leggings, and a T-shirt. Indigo was at the door in no time. I grabbed a bottle of water and a banana and headed out.

"Girl, I have not been in the gym for years. I hope I know what I'm doing." As we walked over to the complex, a lot of people were getting their work out on. I decided to be nosey and see what was going on in the other rooms.

There were a few people getting ready to start their workouts. I guess they were waiting for the instructors to come. I started to look at myself in one of the big mirrors

"I do need to tone up, though I need to get my summer body back," I said as I started to pat my stomach.

"Well summer must already be here, because you already looking good," said a voice behind me.

I looked back with a big smile. "Aww, thank you," I said blushing.

"Hi, how are you? I'm Rocco."

I jumped back. He had such a deep voice. "That's a different name. Never heard that one before.

"It means tough as nails and hard as a rock," he said with authority, while making his chest jump. I hate that; it's not cute, but whatever makes him happy, fine with me. Speaking of fine – that he is. We made eye contact. *Oh, my lord, he has the nicest eyes*, I said to myself.

"Sorry, I didn't catch your name."

"Oh, I'm Naila. Pronounced NYLA. It means successful. That's right, everything I touch will be a success."

"Well, okay then, Miss Naila. So, do you visit this gym frequently?"

"Honestly, no. I'm busy aiming to be successful, but my friend upstairs invited me, and I promised I was going to come with her."

"Girl, will you just get the number and come on?" Indigo yelled.

"I'm sorry, she's in a rush."

"Oh, no problem. Here is my card. You can call me later. Thank you, I sure will."

I didn't even have breakfast or my coffee yet, but I was high just seeing him. Damn! I still can't believe this man was so handsome and humble standing in front of me.

Indigo grabbed me by the hand. "Girl calm down and get it together. Stop lusting over him. I'm sure he has a wife at home, and plus, he is in contact with lots of women here, so be careful. Don't act like you are special. The same way he gave you his number in less than 20 minutes, I'm sure he did the same thing to the other women here. I've seen him around here a few times, but I never paid him any attention. What I do know of him since I've been coming here, he doesn't talk much. He's very intelligent, spiritual, very focused, and private. He comes in, teach his, class and leaves."

"Yeah, with the luck I've been having, I bet you he is married with children. Seems like all the good ones are either married, dead, in jail, or gay. You never know, those silent ones are deadly – very secretive and have something to hide. Wait, what does he teach?"

"Kickboxing."

"Oh nah. I'm all set. Kickboxing is too much for me. I feel like that falls under anger management, to let off some steam; if he can't hit the person at home, he takes it out in the gym. I got to be careful, that's too aggressive for me. That is one class I will not be taking."

I did a little yoga with Indigo, but when we did the floor exercise I dozed off. Hey, I was tired. A few weeks went by. I stayed in touch with Rocco. We hit it off very quickly. I know it was a rebound relationship. We both just wanted to be in each other's company or with anybody since we both just came out of messy marriages. Lord, I thought my prayers had been answered. I started going to the gym more frequently now that my new boo was there, although I never took any of his classes. I'd been dipping into Zumba and Cycling while doing relationship things, including bedroom activities, so I think it was safe for me to say we were a couple. I didn't really tell Indigo all of my business, just that Rocco and I were seeing each other. She just helped me out from a four-year marriage and that was life or death so I wasn't sure what she would say.

I told him, "Let's take it slow. I'm not trying to get locked down again. I need to heal from what my ex-husband put me through."

He passed his finger under my chin and said, "I don't see how any man can hurt a woman." He gave me a whole ten-minute speech on how women should be treated as queens with royalty.

One day, I decided to visit my new boo where he was teaching his kickboxing classes. I walked in the door and tiptoed in the back. He looked at me like he had no idea who I was. I sat in the back of his class while he was teaching. When his class was over, he waited till the room was empty and asked me what the hell was I doing there. "What we have is private. I don't want you popping up on me in front of my class."

I was a little taken aback because we had been spending a lot of time together, going out to dinner, and he was always at my house, in my bedroom, between my sheets, so I was a little shocked. I went back home and put my thinking cap on, not sure if that was an act or Red Flag #1. I wasn't sure if I wanted to continue this relationship if it's going to start off like this.

I texted Indigo: *Hey girl, I'm going to slow down from the gym. Rocco is already showing his ass and I'm not the one.*

My phone had been ringing off the hook

since Rocco had an issue with me popping up in his class. Seven missed calls. Really, dude, what the fuck do you have to say? I continued my text to Indigo: *Girl, I went to his kickboxing class, he is crazy as hell, he has some serious issues; I need to back up from him.*

I started listening to the voicemails: *Where the fuck are you Naila? I am calling you.*

Yo, you better answer the phone the next time I call... matter fact.

I'll be over later so we can finish this conversation.

Boy bye..

I listened to the voice mails and just deleted them. I didn't even return his calls.

Indigo texted back: *Girl, you need to be careful with this one. I just saved your ass from the last psycho you were married to. Seems like that's all you attract.*

I finished cleaning up. I tried to take a nap before he came over. Not knowing this crazy motherfucker was already outside questioning all the tenants to see if they ever seen any men coming in and out my house! Keyword: *my house.*

He knocked on the door. "Who is it?" I asked.

"Me!"

"Who is me?" I already knew who it was, but hey. As soon as I opened the door, he took me by my hand and led me to the couch to sit down.

"I'm sorry about earlier with the crazy messages. I was worried about you. I felt bad when you left, and I don't want to lose you. I should have never acted like that. Please accept my apology," he begged.

"Whatever, Rocco. I see you can do what you want to do, but you want to have me on a leash. I'm not a dog. I'm not going to accept or tolerate this controlling behavior. I refuse to let you take me back to where I just prayed my way out of. You do not control me. That's why when you met me, I was single for a reason. You and I are dating to see if I want to continue on with you, but the way you're acting, I'm not sure."

Why did I say that? His anger went from 1 to 100. I saw a line in the middle of his forehead. I thought he was about to head-butt me. I jumped back. He grabbed me around my neck and pushed me down into the couch. I started kicking him off so he could get his hands from around my neck. He finally let up. I had to catch my breath and gasp for air.

"Yo, what the fuck is your problem, dude?"

Before he could answer, there was a

knock on the door. I wasn't expecting anyone, but I got up to open the door. Plus, I needed to leave.

"Hey, you want to go to the grocery store with me?" Indigo asked. I was about to ask Rocco for permission, but I'm a grown ass-woman. I pay my bills. I don't have to ask him shit. I grabbed my keys, my phone, and walked out the door. Let him sit there and figure out what he is doing. I never told Indigo how many times he hit me or what just happened because I knew she would go upside his head. Indigo is a quiet one but do not get her on her wrong side; she will cut you and watch you bleed.

"Listen, Indigo, I'm missing my family. I only started dating this dude in May and it's November. I think I need to go visit my family in Texas for Thanksgiving to get away from him and spend time with them. I know if I tell him he's going to think I'm lying, but he'll be fine. I'm only telling you this, not him. Plus, you are going to be with your family in Connecticut anyway."

"Girl, do what you have to do as long as you are happy. Stop worrying about a man who can't do shit for you but lay you on your back and stress you out."

"Thanks, girl, I needed that."

We were at the store for about 30 minutes. Rocco texted and said "emergency." I knew it wasn't a damn thing wrong, he just wanted me to rush home. I texted back: *If it's an emergency then call 911.*

Since I was already out, I called my family and told them I was coming down for the holidays and booked my ticket online. They were so excited to see me and, no he was not invited. My family did not like him; they never heard one positive thing about him. He started making Thanksgiving plans. I don't know why and with whom. I wouldn't be there. He claimed he had no family; his ex-wife took their daughter and left, and he didn't know where they went. I came back home and showered and went to sleep. He decided to come layup with me, and that's all he did was lay there. That shit he just pulled earlier did not give him access to me. He ran that "I'm sorry" BS, but I wasn't hearing it.

I booked an evening flight because I knew he had his last kickboxing class and the gym was closing early before the Thanksgiving break. I knew exactly what I was doing. However, I totally forgot everyone and their mama travels for the Thanksgiving holidays.

My Uber showed up on time. I looked outside and checked to see if Mr. Madman was around. I got my suitcase and my bags and locked my door.

I arrived at the airport. I noticed a very long line for flight 1030 to Dallas, Texas. I heard over the intercom my flight was delayed for two hours. So instead of 8:00 pm, it was now for 10:00 pm. I was fine with that, not to mention I never even told him I was going anywhere. I checked my luggage in and made sure everything was ready to go. I decided to have a seat so I could be at peace. I just wanted to take a power nap and would get up in time to board my flight.

    I sat down in the hard chair they provided, put my shades on, and closed my eyes for a bit just to get my mind at ease. I guess today is the day to drive me crazy, because all the babies were crying at the same time. I know it wasn't even 20 minutes, when I felt a body sitting next to me, shoulder to shoulder. I took my shades off and looked over to see who felt the need to sit that close to me. To my surprise, it was Rocco. My heart almost came out of my chest. He spoke very softly in my ear, "You have five minutes to get up, get your bags, and meet me outside or else!!!!" With a threat like that, and knowing from past experience, I knew that he meant business. I totally forgot he had a tracking device on my phone.

    I got up and grabbed my bags. I noticed a security guard standing there and I figured this is my time. I mean, they are there to protect and serve. I started to scream, "Someone please help me, he is trying to kill me." I looked directly at the guard. Everyone heard me, but I was not important to them, so no one helped me or paid me any attention.

The security guard said, "Ma'am, please stop the noise."

I kept screaming, "If I go with him, he will keep beating me. I need help." No one took me seriously because he was already out the door. So, I looked like a madwoman talking to myself. I refused to go outside. The airport was crowded and noisy. I'm sure they were used to crazy things happening.

I guess Rocco was mad I was taking too long, so he came back in and dragged me out the door. Now my thing is, what the fuck? It's a crowed airport, yet no one helped me. I tried to fight with all my strength, but he was bigger than me. I couldn't believe that no one was trying to help me.

I made up my mind, this was it... I kept grabbing onto the door with one hand and my bags in the other hand, while he was grabbing me by the arm with a seriously tight grip. Parents were grabbing their children and blocking their eyes from the scene. A taxi driver with a very strong accent told him to let me go, that is not how you treat a woman. Rocco told him to mind his business. The taxi driver tried to break us apart but got tossed out of the way. He finally got me in the car and started punching me in my face, slapping me with one hand while driving fast with the other. "Where the fuck you think you were going and didn't tell me, ha?"

You would think with a crowded airport someone could have called the police and helped me. I'm wondering what the fuck I did to make this man so angry. What is going through his big head to keep beating me like this? I wanted to jump out the car, but if you ever been to an airport roadway you know it's back to back traffic so if I jumped, I was definitely getting run over by the car behind. The taxi driver followed his car while calling the police; he described the car and a description of Rocco's short brown-skinned, bald head, and about 210 pounds. He told the police where to meet him. The police drove up behind him in an unmarked car and pulled him over at the stop light. This was the only time I didn't care if the police officers' guns went off and killed him, because I wanted to live. I was so afraid of him; he said let him do the talking when the police came out the car. The officer told him to pull over and take the keys out of the ignition.

All I wanted was to catch a flight to see my family, not be on a police chase. Rocco waited till the officer got out of the car and took off.

I was wondering how I got from the airport to playing grand theft auto, because he was swerving between cars, running red lights. I'm sure he did this before, because he outran the officer like a pro. We ended up in the parking lot in my apartment complex. I knew what was about to happen once I got in that house. It was another ass whipping. As we were getting out of the car, I texted Indigo: *COME NOW*. As soon as I pressed send, she was at my door in about a minute.

"Hey girl, I need to make a midnight run and I need some company. Come take a drive with me." That's a code we use when I need to get away. As soon as she saw my face, she rolled her eyes at him and walked away to her car.

Since no other plans were working, I knew it was time for me to step up my game and make my big escape to save my life.

"Girl, do I need to take you to the police station to talk to make a report?"

"No, I don't want to go. I'm not ready for this."

"Girl, you will never be ready. You will keep going back to him over and over again. When he kills you, it will be too late. If you want us to remain friends, you will go now. Get your ass in the car."

Rocco could see us talking but couldn't hear what we were saying. I took my pocketbook out of his car and jumped in Indigo's car. I looked in the mirror. I touched my swollen face. "Ouch, that hurts."

"Well, what do you expect when someone bangs your face into a wall?" she said. She turned the car on. "What the fuck is really going on, Naila? Six months you been with this man and he's beating your ass already?"

"Girl, if I told you what just happened you would not believe it."

She threw her hands up like whatever. We drove at least ten minutes. Mary J Blige's song *No More Drama* was playing in the background. What a coincidence. We pulled up to a building with no name.

"Where the hell are we going? I thought you said we were going to the police station?"

"Listen, the police will ask a lot of questions and give you a restraining order that does not work. Where I'm taking you, people take action. Just follow my lead," she said.

"Okay, miss boss lady. Let's go." I got out of the car, looked around, and put my shades back on. "Okay, let's go. This place looks creepy, but okay, and what the hell is a place like this doing open this time of the night?"

It looked like an old department store that had been remodeled.

"It's for people like you, Naila. Domestic violence is not 9:00 to 5:00, it's 24 hours. It happens all the time and any time. You better thank God it didn't close at 5:00 or I'd be helping your family make funeral arrangements."

We walked up to the front door and waited to get buzzed in. "Are you going to talk, or do I need to talk for you?"

"Hello, how may I help you ladies?"

"Hi, my name is Indigo. I'm here with a friend who needs help. She's being abused at home by her boyfriend and she needs help now before he kills her."

"Can she speak for herself?" asked the young woman at the front desk.

"Whether she can speak for herself or not, you got the story, right?" Indigo said with an attitude.

"Hi, ma'am. Please fill out this form and I will call a domestic violence advocate and they can speak to you. Would you like that?" She looked in my direction.

"Yes, I would. Thank you," I replied softly. My jaw was hurting from those back to back punches.

The secretary phoned for an advocate.

"Please have a seat. Someone will be with you shortly. The five minutes I sat in the waiting room was like an hour. I was in so much pain. I didn't even care if he was tracking my phone. I knew he thought I was at the store with Indigo.

A tall black woman walked up from the back. "Hi, I'm Mya Durante, an advocate for domestic violence. I heard you need help with a situation at home. Please come with me," she said as she walked to the back.

"I'll be in the car. Text me when you are done," Indigo said.

"Okay, I will."

"So, what brings you in here? Sorry, I didn't get your name."

"It's Naila. I'm sorry, you said your last name was Durante. Wow, what a coincidence. That's my boyfriend's last name."

We went into her office. "OMG, your office is so warm and relaxing. I love the setup."

"Please have a seat and thank you very much. My office is where I do a lot of thinking and preparing for myself and my next client. Well, first of all, I'm glad you took the first step to getting help. Don't feel embarrassed for wanting to get a better life and get away from your abuser," Mya said as she closed the door and put up a "do not disturb" sign.

"No one has the right to abuse you at all.

No excuses. Answer these questions for me. Did you fill out the forms in the front?"

"No, I just sat down to fill it out and you came out."

"Okay, we can go over it together. What are you prepared to do?" Mya asked.

"I'm just here to see what is the process of leaving and how to leave without him knowing? Well, it's my house. I'm not leaving. I mean, to leave this relationship. My mouth and face hurts from an incident we had two hours ago."

"Do you have a place to go right now if you leave tonight?"

"Nope. I can't stay with my friend. She lives upstairs; he will know that's where I am."

"So, where are your family and friends?"

"They are in Texas. Our conversation is limited due to him. I was on my way to go see my family and he tracked my phone and found out where I was, and the rest is history."

"Listen here, you sound like you want to leave, then you sound like you don't. You have to know in your heart if you want to leave so we can put things in place for you. You are here now; you don't have to go back."

"It's my house. I am going back. He needs to leave," I shouted.

"I can take you to get a restraining order."

"Well, I don't even know where he lives to serve him, he's always at my house or the gym. And I'm not leaving my house to make him comfortable. I can't stay long here; he will look for me and if he finds me, he will start beating me again," I said as I burst out in tears. "I really want this to be over and done with. I don't have the energy to go through this. I really don't want a "stay away order" of protection or a restraining order. None of those things work; if it did, we would have less women dying from domestic violence. It triggers them more and they start with the threats. He has a tracker on my phone. Right now, he thinks I'm at the store with my friend."

"Listen, Naila. Do you want to know why I became an advocate?"

"Truth be told, nope, not really. I'm tired of hearing everyone's heroic stories, but if you must, share it. Go ahead." I sat up in the chair to give her my attention.

"I lost my daughter to domestic violence. My ex-husband came home drunk and started slapping me around, as usual, blaming me for his bad day. My 12-year-old daughter got tired of seeing him hit me and she stepped in. She tried to push him away from me. He lost it. He had so much rage and built-up anger in him. He stabbed her 14 times. He got up, dropped the knife, and walked out the door. He got in his car and drove off. Police were called. They almost got him but he kept putting his car in reverse and forward. He caused complete chaos. They almost cornered him, but he took them on a wild, high speed chance and just disappeared."

Okay, wait a minute. Why does she sound like she's telling my story? I said to myself. This is the exact thing I went through with this crazy ass I'm with.

Mya continued, "We have not seen or heard from him since. Even at the funeral I looked around and thought he would show his face. His picture was all over the news, but he still has not been found. Today makes it three years since I buried my daughter. I went to the cemetery this morning. I wanted to stay home and cry all day, but God told me to go to work because another woman needs me and here you are, sitting in front of me."

"Wow, what a story. You are very strong and courageous. I wish I was strong like you," I said.

"And you could be," said Mya.

Mya showed me the scars on her arm where she was shielding her face from the knife but ended up getting cut on her arm instead. "That was the worst feeling in the world, to bury my child because of the man I chose to marry." She took out two pictures from her top desk drawer. "Look, this is my daughter and this is the man who killed her."

I swear I saw a ghost. I did a double take at the second picture.

"I'm sorry, what did you say his name was?" I asked.

"His name is Erick Durante, but he goes by the name Rocco. Everyone says he acts and looks like a pit bull; that's where he got the name from."

I wanted to cry and run out the door at the same time, because everything she said sounded exactly like Rocco. Well, it is! I inhaled and let out a deep breath.

Mrs. Durante continued. "I took myself to school and decided I was going to help other women for my daughter, so please let me help you. If you walk out that door now and go back to him, you might not make it back to file a restraining order. I do not want to hear another woman lost her life by someone she loves. Are you listening to me?"

"Yeah." I had to catch myself from the time I saw his picture. My mind was in the red zone. Because if he can kill an innocent child in front of her mother, what can he do to me?

The picture she showed me was Rocco,

the only difference was in the picture, he had dreads and was about 350 pounds, so it's kind of hard to notice him now, that's why they never found him. But I am going to get that little girl justice.

"Thanks, ma'am. I'll take your card and I promise I will call you if I need you. Thanks for listening." I got up, pushed my chair in, and walked right out the door.

Mya followed behind me. "Don't make me read about you in the newspaper, young lady."

"You won't," I yelled back as the door closed.

Indigo was laying back in her driver's seat when she heard a tap on her glass. She opened the door. "So how was it? That was quick."

"It was good. Very informative. She told me her story. I told her mine, but I walked out and decided to give him another chance."

"Girl, please tell me you are playing," she said as she sat up in the driver's seat.

"No, I'm serious, Indigo."

"You know what? Let me drive your ass back home to your man. If I don't see you tomorrow, I'll know what happened. This man is tracking your phone, beating your ass, I can't see you unless he says so. And it's only six months."

I had a plan; I just wasn't telling them. When you tell people what you are about to do, they want to talk you out of it.

Rocco was already tracking my phone. He knew I did not go to the store. But I never said that was my destination. He was peeping out the window to see when I was going to pull up and get out of Indigo's car. He heard a door slam, laughing and talking. He ran back to the couch to pretend he was watching TV. He heard the key in the door. I didn't even step foot in the door, he asked, "How was your midnight run?"

"It was fine," I said in a low voice.

"I'm gonna ask you one more motherfucking time, and if I catch you lying, I'm gonna fuck you up. HOW THE FUCK WAS YOUR MIDNIGHT RUN?" he yelled as he walked over to me.

My mind was on Mya's daughter. All the women who died from domestic violence. All the blows I took from him. The airport. What my ex-husband put me through. What I just came out of, not to mention all the embarrassing moments from him. Indigo had a feeling something was about to go down, because she never even went upstairs, plus I didn't say much in the car. My blood was boiling. I was angry and furious.

STOP

He slapped me so hard in my mouth, I jumped back. I took the little bit of strength I had left in me and pushed his 210-pound ass away from me. "Excuse me, who the fuck you think you hitting?" I yelled at him.

"You bitch!" He was surprised that I even spoke back. He slammed the door and made sure it was locked in Indigo's face. He reached over and grabbed my neck from behind and pushed me into the kitchen. The first thing my eyes saw was a knife. I grabbed it with my right hand and turned around and stabbed him in his stomach. He jumped back.

"What the fuck you doing, you crazy bitch?"

"I got your crazy bitch," I said as I lunged towards him with the knife, while wiping the blood from my mouth. "I told you before – the next motherfucker put his hands on me will be a dead motherfucker and I'm not playing."

He attempted to slap me again, but as soon as he swung, I sliced his wrist. "Keep coming. The closer you come to me the less chance you have of being alive." I waved the knife at him.

I knew Indigo was helpless, because she couldn't do anything but listen to the chaos through the doors.

"Now you have two choices: call the police or I'll be calling your mother to come claim your body. Pick one."

Rocco stood there surprised with his hands over his stomach. He removed his hands and noticed the blood was coming through his shirt, which only made him more upset. He realized he didn't have all that power. After all, he was standing there watching me as I held the knife in my hand. I knew if I let go, I was going to be carried out in a body bag. One of us would be dead tonight and it wasn't gonna be me.

"Yo, put the knife down. Let's talk," he said calmly.

"Talk about what? For once, y'all motherfuckers need to know what it's like to get hit or punched and stabbed. I bet you don't like it, ha?" I started to hit him with the other side of the knife. It finally broke and fell out of my hand. He thought he had me when he grabbed both hands and tried to push me back against the wall. I bit him on his hand and kicked him between his legs until he went down, begging for me to stop. He lost his balance and fell to the floor. I kept stomping him for every time he hit me and I couldn't hit back. "Take that for all the abuse, pain and torture you put me through." I kneeled down close to him. I whispered in his ear, "That was also for the little 12-year-old child you killed when you were beating her mother's ass. You punk bitch." Rocco looked puzzled, wondering how I knew about that incident.

"Naila, are you alright?" I heard Indigo yell from the hallway followed by lots of banging. "Open the door," she yelled.

"I can't. Call the cops," I yelled.

"I already did. They are on their way."

In less than two minutes, the police were at the door. I jumped up and ran to the door. As I tried to turn the knob, it broke. I was in pain and so weak and exhausted, I didn't have any fight in me. I tried to rattle the door for it to open. I yelled and told the officers, "Kick down the door. He will kill me. Hurry, he will kill me."

Within five seconds they kicked down the door and saw him lying on the floor, pointing to his stomach. "She stabbed me, she stabbed me."

"Yup, you damn right I stabbed you, because you were coming at me with the knife. It was either you or me, and I told you I was not going to die by the hands of no man."

A few minutes later the ambulance arrived and asked me was I okay. "Yes, I'm fine. A little bruised up, but I'll be fine. He needs medical attention, not me," I said, as I pointed to him. We were both transferred to different hospitals.

I spent two whole days crying and healing. The nurse brought my discharge papers along with two special guests. With no introduction, I hugged Mya so tight. "Hey, I'm proud of you for fighting back. I thought he was going to kill you, but I'm glad you defended yourself. I was so worried about you when you walked out of my office. I knew something triggered you when you saw his picture."

"How did you know I was here?" I asked.

"You left my card in your friend's car and she called while everything was going on. She told me she already called the police and there's only one hospital in your area. Naila, listen, you did us all a favor. You helped me close old pain and solved my daughter's case while protecting yourself."

"Will I get locked up?"

"You can claim self-defense, girl, trust me. I can tell them you came to me looking for help. You have witnesses and scars to show."

"Listen, Mya, the reason I left your office so fast when I saw the picture of Rocco, then your daughter, was because everything hit me all at once. I knew I had to fight for her. I need to go home, take a bubble bath, and soak in the tub. My body is so sore."

My ride or die friend walked in. "Hey girl, I'm so proud of you. You have no idea how helpless I was. I didn't know what his crazy ass was going to do. Let's make a deal, no more dating for at least two years," she laughed. Indigo hugged me so tight.

"It's nice to have my best friend and my life back."

"Let's go home and get some sleep and track down your suitcase tomorrow. Matter of fact, you have a lot to be thankful for, so you will be spending Thanksgiving with me and my family."

I slept all the way. When we got to my complex, I looked at my door and just shook my head. I went straight upstairs to Indigo's apartment just like the old days. Watching movies, eating junk food, chilling like besties.

It feels so good not being disrespected or getting hit or beaten for nothing. I did call my family and told them everything, they were heartbroken, but felt better that he was no longer in the picture. He's already getting life in prison without parole for the murder of his ex-wife's daughter and being a fugitive on the run; that was enough and I didn't feel like anything I said would have made a difference.

Personal note from me: If you see the first red flag, get out right away. Not all women will survive domestic violence relationships. I don't want you to come out in a body bag. My goal is for you to come out better than when you went in. I want you to come out empowered, motivated to do better, and learn more about yourself, what you will accept and you will not accept.

Domestic violence is never okay. Don't ever try to take matters into your own hands. Seek help. Get out. Don't think he or she will change unless they can get the help they seriously need.

STOP

WHY

Why are you putting your hands on me?
This is not how I imagined my life to be.
How did I end up with you?
I'm tired of my skin turning black and blue.
I walked away because I know I deserve
better; in a perfect world
I will get love and happiness.
If I stay with you
it will only be sadness and bitterness.
I'm tired of fighting for my life. I never
planned to be an abused wife.
I started to make excuses for you. I started
to cover the scars and the bruises, started to
blame myself for your sickness.
Then I stopped.
I stopped because I deserve better.
I got tired of collecting hospital bracelets.
What happened to the days
when couples argue, disagree, followed by
candy and flowers, I wonder?
Now the only time I see flowers
is when she's six feet under.
Please give me flowers and roses now
because you love me.
Don't bring it to my funeral
because you miss me.

I GET IT

I'm sorry it had to be you. I'm sorry that he turned your body black and blue.

I'm sorry he wasn't raised not to put his hands on a woman, when he clearly came from a woman. I get it, I know you were looking for love, but listen to me, if these men don't have love, or know how to love, how do you expect them to give love to you, or me, or anybody else? See, we need to start reading the big black book on the shelf. Yea, that's right, the Bible, because right now, our minds are idle. And you know an idle mind is the devil's playground. We got to stop this cycle from going around and round.

I get it, he buys you nice things. He gives you money, he loves his kids, he pays the bills. Ladies, please stop giving a man credit for what he is supposed to do. He is good in bed; he worships the ground you walk on. He said till death do us part. Yup, he was right, till death do you part. Because the same family you tried to keep together has now been torn apart.

Why do some women believe that it's

okay to be living in hell?

With a man that beats your ass and then give you roses you can't smell.

Yeah, I know on the past you can't dwell.

But his ass needs to be in a cell.

A man that controls you mentally, physically, sexually, emotionally, spiritually, can do what he wants to do and get away with it eventually.

'Leave before it's too late.' I did and I feel great.

The moment he hit you after he had a drink, then you become the weakest link.

For all my survivors, this advice you should take; please don't make this same mistake.

I WAS THAT WOMAN

I know this woman who is being held against her will by her boyfriend or husband. She wants to come out. The only time she comes out is when she is being wheeled out in an ambulance from when she accidentally ran into a wall, (bullshit he pushed her) or when she didn't see the toy on the floor and she fell (more lies again, he punched her so hard she fell down the stairs). She's depressed, because she goes to bed every night, crying and wishing she could get out, but she can't. She already gave her life to this man; she gave up her family and friends to live this fairytale life he promised her that turned into a nightmare. After he beats her and she's lying on the bed, he comes over and says, "You know I didn't mean it right? You made me do it." Then he tells her he loves her. Oh boy, here he comes, wiping her tears away. The same tears he caused her to cry, and she fell right back into the trap of spreading her legs to him because he loves her all over again. See, he only loves her until something doesn't go his way and he takes it out on her again.

STOP

I know this woman who does not want to get out of bed because her husband asked for sex and she refused, so he grabbed her by one hand, dragged her into the room, threw her on the bed and took it from her, as she screams to the top of her lungs, "Stopppp!" Her four-year-old son woke up from hearing the screaming, he opened the room door and saw his father on top of his mother, her pants down to her ankles. Her husband got up and shut the door; this time he locked it and continued forcing himself inside of her. She kept screaming until he covers her mouth so she would be quiet. But after a while she stopped falling for his games, she got tired of her eyes being black, her body being bruised, her bones being broken, and her son being traumatized.

I know there is a woman who is sick and tired of being sick and tired, fed up with all men because this one guy did the same thing to her the last one did, but said "I'm not like the rest." She puts on that fake smile and her superwoman cape, standing in a room full of people. Her exterior is strong, resilient and fierce. But inside she's frustrated, angry and broken. She walks away, sits in her car, tilts her head back on the headrest, and the tears started flowing like a nonstop running faucet. She's praying to God to turn her sorrow into joy and her tears into laughter. She's tired, she's fed up, and she's had enough.

See, I know there is a woman sitting here reading this, and her eyes are flooded with tears. She wants to cry because she knows one of those women, maybe she is that woman. Well if you are that woman, it's time to stop being held back. It's time to kick down the door and escape that life; this was not part of God's plan. Instead of lying there asking, "Why me?" Stand up tall and strong, put that smile on your face, and say "Why not try me?" Get up and fight, let him know you are done, you are tired, you will not take this anymore. No man has the right to hold you hostage; no man has the right to control you or put his hands on you. No man has the right to take you for granted.

You have a voice inside of you. You have to reach a point in your life where you know when it's time to walk away from a toxic relationship. Do not stay in a toxic relationship just because others are telling you to do so. If you know in your heart this is not what is right for you, be strong enough to walk away. ABUSE does not equal LOVE. If he beats you and then says "sorry" and then beats you all over again, that is not love. Walking away is hard, but it is a fresh start to be loved by someone who truly loves you. Do not stay in a relationship just for the sake of the children or to put on a show for friends and family.

I SIT AND WAIT

I sit and wait for you to get home, hoping that you'll be in a good mood, knowing that in the end, it won't make a difference.

I sit and wait, watching your moves, knowing that you'll find some reason to fight with me or blame me for something I didn't do. Here comes the screaming, the yelling, the blaming. I'm so used to the bullshit.

I keep wondering why you keep apologizing, yet you keep doing the same shit over and over again, as if you don't know any better, but then again you don't.

I was waiting for the neighbors to knock on the door to ask for sugar or milk or something so I can answer it, so they can see my face and call the police, but you always answer the door and tell them I'm not home or I'm sleeping. Good move.

I did an inventory on my body so I can count and see how many scars or bruises I have, what's old and what's new. It's my new hobby.

I was waiting to see if the sleeping pills I put into your drink actually worked so you can be knocked out. It will be my only chance to escape. Well what do you know? It worked. You slept like a baby and I was able to walk out the door, and when you woke up, that's right.... your punching bag was gone.

I waited for you to change. I figured you would come to your senses, but you didn't. I had to come to my senses. I couldn't help myself then, but I could now.

People ask why victims stay in abusive relationships.

They need to ask why abusers keep abusing.

Guess what? The waiting game is over.

No more waiting, no more bruising, no more hits, no more abuse.

I left. I had to. I wanted to be happy, and that I am.

I can't tell you how I really feel. You don't care anyway, you will not change, you will continue doing what you always do, get mad and ignore me.

I can't do the things I really want. You held me back and said I will never make it in this world. I can't talk to you about my dreams, my goals, or my visions. You never believed in me, so I gave them up.

I couldn't see the light; your darkness was too overpowering.

I can't live like I want; you criticize everything I do, everything I do is a problem. Everything I do is stupid or dumb; I'm lazy when I'm home. I get two jobs, now I am a hoe. You made me quit my job because you claim I'm screwing everyone on the job. I don't have any money; you emptied my bank account for you and your outside woman. I can't talk on the phone because I'm cheating.

I can't take this anymore, but what I can do is get up and walk away.

P.S. I do feel sorry for the next woman you end up with, unless you get help for your anger issues, no woman will be good enough for you.

STOP

I WILL BE YOUR VOICE

*A person with no voice cannot be heard.
I'm not going to keep turning my head
and not say a word.
I can't pretend I don't see
that woman on the floor.
She could have been me, or you,
your mother, your sister, your daughter.
When you hit one woman,
you hit all when you put your hands on her.
I feel the pain when she falls.
I help her back up on her feet
to stand strong.
To all the women who have been hit
and can't speak,
I'll be your voice.
To all the women who are still
in an abusive relationship, get out now.
To all the women that want to get out
or need to get out,
do me a favor and break free,
walk away and don't look back.*

I am a woman; I have to do my part. I can't sit here and listen to these stories. I have to speak up and spread the message. If I save a life, then I served my purpose.

Over the years I was able to bless a lot of stages and airwaves. I touched so many lives. I now know how many men and women that were hurting and were afraid to speak up. I decided to put together a collection of poems for victims and survivors regarding sexual abuse and domestic violence.

I don't think people fully understand what happens to anyone who's been abused, physically, emotionally, sexually, mentally, verbally, even spiritually. People don't know it can destroy your entire life. I had to look in the mirror and realized I am worth it, I deserve better, I have a purpose, I need to live, and I have a story to tell. My abusers already did the damage; now I have to put the pieces of my shattered life back together. I started writing to deal with my pain, and now with the release of my book, I am able to do that. People now understood why I didn't want to live anymore. Until you have walked the miles I have walked, and your feet can fit perfectly in my shoes, then you can talk. I cried every night when I go to sleep. Tears are a language only the almighty God can understand. You see the jokes, the smiles, the positive posts on social media. No one knew what I was dealing with every day. I never allowed anyone in my circle. I suffer with migraine headaches, endometriosis, fibromyalgia, vertigo, anxiety,

PTSD, and numerous nervous breakdowns. My last four relationships were the worst; they all turned out to be domestic violence. I lost everything (my house, my businesses). I had to rebuild.

Every morning I thank God for allowing me to wake up to see another day. I get mad at the disappointments, but I laugh because I know whatever I lost, I am getting back so much greater. I will always be grateful. I will always stand strong and not complain because I am truly blessed. It don't matter what I have been through. My God will not give me more than I can bear. Learning to let go and forgive was the best part of this journey.

A LETTER TO MY ABUSIVE EXES

In order for me to start living a stress-free life, I must let go of this pain. I just couldn't believe that I was a victim over 25 years. I find myself saying "my ex did this, and he did that." I kept that going for months straight; it was all about them. It drove me crazy that I was hurt repeatedly. Today I can talk without even mentioning my ex. Now I can live a stress-free life.

Dear Ex . . . I was about to say I don't even know where to start with this letter, but I do. In order for me to completely move on, I have to release this pain. See, I never got a chance to confront you about how you were treating me. I never argued back; I just took the blows, the insults, the disrespect, the lies, and the cheating. I simply walked away, accepted my losses, and moved on. I just need to let this out because I need to let go and move on with my life.

Please listen, I'm not even mad at you. I thank you for what you put me through, which gave me the strength to walk away from you. I'm glad you pushed me away. They say everything happens for a reason and I never understood what it meant, but I understand it now. See, if you didn't ignore me, treat me bad and push me away, I wouldn't be smiling now. I wouldn't be happy. I see you watching me from afar, I see you adding me on Facebook and wanting to follow me on social media, but when I was with you, I couldn't be on social media. Everything you did to me made me stronger and better. I had to let you know you didn't break me. You didn't appreciate what you had in front of you, but someone else did, so again, I thank you.

Dear Ex . . . Thank you for showing me how strong I am. For me to go through this, I had to be strong. Eight years has passed, and today I can smile again. No one knew what was going on, why I was broken. Every time I stood up for myself, I was knocked down again by you. To wake up every morning not knowing when will be my last day with you was sick. But you made me a stronger person. I told you what I already went through, not to take me there again, but you took me through worse. Thank you, because without that I wouldn't know the pain of being abused and lied to. I wouldn't be able to help others going through it. If I didn't hit the floor, I would not be able to bounce back up.

You seriously broke me down. From being a model, you said I was a hoe; you said I was ugly, but you were with me. You needed me; I did not need you. I was taking care of you. I was investing in you. I am a firm believer in God, and I knew if I held on to the faith I had, I was going to get out of it. You kept pulling me back every time I got higher in life; clearly you were the problem, not me. Thank you for showing me how strong I am.

I remembered one day we were arguing because you said you were going to take me out after me sitting in the house all week doing nothing, while you ran the streets. I was ready and waiting. I remembered you went in the bathroom and asked someone to call you in five minutes. You walked out of the bathroom into the room. Your phone rang all of a sudden. You lied and told me that you were on call; it was your job calling. You had to leave for a while, all because you wanted to be with the other woman, you left me in the house to cheat with her and she called me and told me you were on your way there. You tried to come back to me but once you left so did I. Thank you for kicking me out of your house on Valentine's Day, the day I looked forward to. I guess that was my answer to the question, did you ever love me? I would watch the TV shows about how these so-called men abuse their women. I called them stupid for staying, but being in their shoes, I know they don't want to stay, they did not know how to get out. What I don't get is how can you take me away from my friends and family and then treat me like a slave?

You shouted at me in the streets and called me stupid. You always talked down to me in front of your friends and made me feel so small. You slapped me across the face at the bus stop. People looked on and didn't help; people were looking at you like you were crazy to see a beautiful black woman like me standing with an ugly guy like you. Thank you, because you gave me the drive to carry on with my life and prove you wrong.

I chuckle now to see how you made me feel like I was nothing when I was with you, but sorry to break your heart. I am something with or without you. After I left, I prayed not to see you again, but I saw you last year and you still tried to bring me down. You broke me down slowly over the years. I didn't want to live after we broke up. I did not know how to start another relationship. I was not sure if he was going to do what you did or worse. I wouldn't look for another relationship because I did not want to start over again. I didn't leave the house; I was so scared to see you around. I knew I was going to have an anxiety attack, and it happened.... you popped up at my door. I had three anxiety attacks that day. I wanted to say so much to you, but my mind and body froze up. I knew what I wanted to say but it was not coming out.

You set me up in August to get me killed, but the gun jammed. Then you popped up at my door to finish me off. How does it feel that you tried to kill me twice, now you are doing 25 to life? I hated myself for being so broken and hated myself for the lack of energy to move on or to push myself further. Because something in the back of my head kept telling me "I'm ugly" "I'm no good" "I will never make it" "No man will ever want me." You took everything away from me. I had nothing left.

Dear Ex . . . You told people I was your cousin. You didn't want anyone to know your business. It's hard to take pictures. I don't smile because when you knocked me down to the floor, I hit the concrete and you knocked my tooth out. I lost all my confidence, I stopped doing speaking engagements, I lost friends, I lost book deals, I lost it all, but I got back up. Thank you for the continuous lies and cheating. I learned, boy did I learn how disgusting you were, and probably still are. It proves it was you that had the problem, not me. When you met me, I was a motivational speaker; I had jobs speaking to women, travelling the world. I was well known. I had it going on, enjoying life, but you took that away from me. You said you wanted me to pursue my dreams, but I was accused of sleeping around. But thank you. I'm strong now. I know how to handle things. I'm determined to make a better life for myself. I will remember what you did, how you treated me, and how you abused me. I can and will get over it.

I've done very well for myself. I still have a long way to go and I'm fighting hard with so much anger and depression every day, but I've got the rest of my life to fight for it. I will be somebody, the same person you broke down. You will hear about me as I rise to the top with my faith in God. Yes, it is hard starting over because you emptied me, so now I have to rebuild from the ground up. I pray for you; I pray that you have changed and you do not treat another woman the way you treated me. Well, you don't even have that choice because you are serving time.

I pray another man don't treat your daughter the way you treated me. I pray that you asked God to forgive you for treating me the way you did. You have to ask for forgiveness.

ABOVE IT ALL, IT ENDS TODAY

I spent four years being tortured, abused – mentally, emotionally, physically and sexually by my ex-husband. Like many of us, I wanted a happy marriage and to have a happy life afterward. That never happened. I lived in fear, feeling trapped, desperately looking for any way that I could get out. My ex-husband was set in his ways; he said that's his religion. Four years with him messed me up for life.

Every time I called the police, they would show up but would not arrest him, because he is also an officer, but at a different district. They thought it was a joke; they asked me what I wanted them to do. His friends were number one in his life, it was all about them. I wish he had married them. I couldn't get a restraining order. We lived together.

Eight years later I now have my independence and am living a life free from violence and abuse – I now have the courage to move forward with my life. The kind of life I know I truly deserve.

At the police station, I said, "Good morning, I'd like to fill out a police report **again** please."

Officer Tavi looked up. "Oh, it's you again, Mrs. Thomas."

"Yup, me again, that's right. I'll keep coming here until you put my husband in jail." Officer Tavi said, "Well, you know he was arrested two nights ago, right?"

"You did not arrest him. You go get him, drive around in the car, hang out with him, and then release him, and he is back at it again."

Here came another officer. "Good morning, Mrs. Thomas, my name is Officer Lewis," he said as he reached out his hand to shake mine. I just looked at him up and down and folded my arms. "I regret to inform you that we can no longer keep arresting James."

I walked away and started banging the glass. I knew it. I fucking knew it. Officer Lewis grabbed me from behind so I wouldn't hurt my hands or break the glass. "That means you are giving him the green light to keep abusing me." "Well, Mrs. Thomas, the great thing is you have a restraining order against him," said Officer Lewis.

"What the fuck is so great about a restraining order?" I yelled. "It does not work. It's just a piece of paper, so hold up! If he gets in his mood and decides to kill me, can I pull out the restraining order for him to stop? You can't bring a restraining order to a gun fight, you jackass. Please remember we are married. We live in the same house. How is that going to work? I swear this is the most stupid shit I ever heard in my entire life. This motherfucker can beat me like a rug and walk around like it's okay. It's because he is a cop, he keeps getting off, ha? A piece of paper can't protect me," I shouted.

"Please lower your voice," he asked. I rolled my eyes at him.

Officer Carnegie came over. "Hey, what's going on, Mrs. Thomas?"

"How many officers are going to keep coming in here asking me what's going on? Can't you see? I come here all the time, I report the same abuse, you ask me the same questions. You all need a better line of communication, or compare notes, or something."

"Would you like something to drink, Mrs. Thomas?" asked Officer Carnegie.

"Yes, please, an iced green tea with four sugars."

"Where do you expect me to get it from?"

"So, why did you ask if you don't have it?" I replied.

"Well, I'm sure you want a million dollars, but I don't have it either."

"But I didn't ask for a million dollars. Did y'all really pay to go to school to become officers or it was a free class?" I asked while looking at all three of them. I know they were trying to cheer me up, but I really had enough of the jokes. I was just ready for them to take him away and keep him.

"Everything will be alright," said Officer Carnegie. "I will protect you. I will not allow him to touch you again."

"And what exactly are you going to do to prevent that? I'm listening," I said while I rolled my eyes at him. "Please tell me how you are going to do that? When he gets in his mood, he takes it out on me. I'm here at least once a week. You go out, you find him, you arrest him or take him for a ride in your car, then you release him. So, when you don't see me here again, come find me in the morgue."

"Please stop talking like that," said Officer Carnegie.

I realized I wasn't getting anywhere with this conversation. I walked back out the door and went back home. I knew he was at work, so I could get a rest and a little peace and quiet before he came home early from work to check on me to see who I was with or what I was doing and find another reason to hit me.

I was glad my son always spends the weekend upstairs so he would not be around to see or experience this shit. I made sure he had breakfast and packed his bag for the weekend. He was all set to go chill with his little buddies.

I took a hot shower, got dressed in my sweats and long shirt, grabbed a book, and curled up in the corner on the couch. I kept hearing something vibrating. I remembered the guys were mowing the lawn outside. I ignored the noise and continued reading. I heard it again, now a constant vibrating. I listened closer and realized it was coming out of the first drawer. I opened it and saw a cell phone. How did he leave his phone home, or maybe this is a secret one? I picked it up and saw numerous text messages. The most recent one said: *Are you going to tell her about us?* I felt a cramp in my stomach and took a deep breath. I knew she realized it was read, so she was waiting for a reply.

I pretended to be him. I texted back and said: *There is nothing to tell.*

The person replied back: *Well you should tell her soon before the baby comes or I would drop this baby at your doorstep.*

I had to remember it was me replying and not him, so I had to put my feelings aside and shift myself in a man's zone. I froze. I couldn't think of a comeback. I started scrolling up to check the previous messages. Another one said: *I enjoyed last night with you; I can't wait to see you again.* My eyes opened up a little wider. I forgot the other one was waiting for a reply, so I scrolled back down to that number and replied: *Listen what you and I had is done, I'm all set with you.* A few text messages had no names attached to them, a few had men's names in it. No w either he is gay or thinks I'm stupid. I didn't know if I was coming or going. I deleted my replies to her or him and placed the phone back in the drawer.

My mind flashed back to all the times I've been hurt and lied to by people. I asked myself what I was doing wrong. I had to shake myself out of this crazy thinking. I tried to finish reading but it was too much to digest. I fell asleep on the couch. I guess he came in and grabbed the cell phone, because when I woke up it was gone. I didn't say a word. I didn't call him to ask anything. Just the normal routine. Later on that morning he came in, took a shower, and went out on the balcony with his boys while I was in the room doing nothing. I started realizing this is not what I signed up for.

He came in to use the bathroom and I heard a woman came and yelled out his name. He went outside to her. They were under the window talking. She started demanding money from him as if it was something she always did on a regular basis. He said, "I'll give it to you later." Why is he even giving her money? Wait, I'm the wife! How does another woman have so much authority to demand something from him?

I came out of the room and went outside. (Why did I do that?) I asked, "What's going on? Who is she and why are you giving her money?" Without warning, he slapped me so hard I hit the floor. In fear of what he would do next, I stayed down on the ground.

Everyone in the corridor started laughing. One of his boys said, "That's right, put that b**** in her place."

I tried to get up, one hand holding on to the railing, the other hand protecting my stomach, trying to find my way up on my feet, but he knocked me down again. One of his boys, Edmund, yelled, "Yo, James. Stop."

I got up. My mouth and nose were bleeding. He grabbed me by my neck with his right hand and pushed me up against the wall while my feet were dangling in the air. He said, "Don't you ever disrespect me in front of my boys again, you got that b****?" I was so embarrassed. Our eyes made contact. I could see the hate in his eyes. He dropped me down and I ran in the house. I tried to catch my breath and figure out what the hell just happened.

I already made up my mind I was not going to stay in any relationship where a man was going to keep beating me down like we are in a boxing ring. I'm done. No more of this shit. I collected my thoughts, drank some water, and had enough strength and courage to walk right out the door. Everybody was looking at me like, where is she going? I did not even look back.

I walked right back to the police station. "Listen up, y'all better get me a room in here if I'm always going to be here." The same officers that saw me earlier this morning were just looking at each other like, she is here again. Now that they saw the bloody nose and the tears, they might take me seriously. I walked over and sat on the cold, hard, wooden bench. "This place smells like pee," I said.

I could see that Officer Tavi really wanted to help but there was only so much he could have done. He gave me a towel to wipe my nose and a bottle of water. I guess I was supposed to drink it, but I poured it on the towel and wiped my bloody nose.

He told me to sit here for as long as I wanted and when I'm ready let him know. I never let him know, because I was never ready to leave. Where would I go? I saw men and women coming in, being booked on different charges. All I could do was shake my head. One lady was dragged in, handcuffed, with blood all over her. I tried to listen in to hear what's going on, but there was so much going on with the radios, scanners, and phones ringing. I could tell she was in a fight. I found out she got tired of the abuse and stabbed her boyfriend. He was in the hospital, but she was being booked on assault charges. Men can beat us and kill us; they get to go to anger management class. But when we fight back, we get locked up and thrown in jail. I guess we are not supposed to defend ourselves.

    I need to find a way to make a change in this world for victims like her and myself. I nodded my head to give her hope. I made a love heart with my hands for her, letting her know I feel her pain. She nodded back at me. I got up and went back to the desk.

    Officer Carnegie escorted me into a room with two chairs and a table to make sense of this situation.

    "So, what's the next step? I feel like this is my second home."

    "Well, we can get you a victim's advocate, someone who you will be able to speak to one-on-one about any and everything. They will be able to put you up. He or she can come in once a week to make sure you are getting the help you need."

"Please make sure it's a woman. I hate men," I interrupted.

"Okay, well, I will put that in my notes. As I was saying, they can get you all the help you need. Finding a safe place, getting back to school or work, they can also sign you up to take Domestic Violence classes."

"Wait! Why am I taking classes? He is the abuser. I am the victim. He needs help. I didn't do shit to him. Is there some kind of protection code or favoritism going on, because no matter what I say you'll keep protecting him?"

"Mrs. Thomas, how can I put this?" He put his finger on his chin. "Honestly, we are starting to think you have some psychological problems. You are here at least once a week."

I jumped up in his face. "Listen, jackass. I'm asking for help. I'm begging for help. I don't have a phone. I can't go outside. I have no one to talk to, so when I do escape and come down here, trust me, I'm looking for help. Psychological problems, ha." I got up and pushed the table over on him. "You think I'm crazy, I'm going to show you fucking crazy." I knocked all the papers out of his hand onto the floor.

Two other officers came in and held me down. I started screaming like a maniac. They called for backup and an ambulance. While I was being dragged out of the room, I kept kicking everything in sight. Officer Tavi asked what the hell just happened. I flipped out, that's what happened. It seems like you have to act crazy to get help these days. They called an ambulance for me and held me there until it arrived. They strapped me down for my safety and medicated me.

All I knew is I woke up drowsy in a mental hospital. I must say, the medication made me feel better. I felt a sense of calm when I woke up. A lot of people came in to ask 101 questions. Please give me a break, I need to collect my thoughts and figure out what happened.

I was invited to participate in groups and counseling. I declined. I got my own issues; I don't need to hear anybody else's. The kind of help I need, they can't give it to me. While there, I was diagnosed with borderline depression, PTSD, anxiety and stress. Maybe I should have been a doctor, because I already knew that. If you have a man beating your ass for nothing, and the police are on his side, what the fuck do you expect?

I was in a tiny room with a little tiny bed, and of course, a TV. Nothing else was in the room. No problem. Anywhere is better than going back home. They had me listed as borderline suicidal; an officer was placed outside my door for protection. Like where the hell will I go and why would I kill myself? The nurses came in every hour. They were nice; they didn't say much, just asked me to verify my name and date of birth, then gave me my pills. Every time I lay down, I ended up crying, so I got out of my bed, walked over to the big window, looking like my 50-inch TV at the house. Got to be careful, don't want them to think I wanted to jump or kill myself.

Looking out the window, having a talk with myself, watching the construction workers down at the bottom doing their work, I remembered the flowers, the cards, the roses, the long conversations.

He told me he loved me, and he will never hurt me. Where did it go wrong? This is not what I signed up for. How did I end up in this mess?

I'm supposed to be a strong, happy, positive, woman.

People look up to me, I'm teaching women not to allow a man to hit or abuse them and here I am, I can't even practice what I preach.

I have to do better; I must get out of here.

I got to fix myself; I have to help other women in my situation.

It ends today. "I don't want to die." I just

started living. If I go back home, he will kill me. Please, I don't want to die. I have a son; I want to see him graduate and get married. I'm not weak, I'm not a punk. I can do this; no, I'm going to do it. I want to make a difference in the world. If I die, I will be a victim. If I live, I will be a survivor.

"You're not going to die. Stop it," said a voice behind me. I guess I was too busy motivating myself, I didn't hear the knock. I turned around to see who was entering my room. A tall black woman, very well dressed, with a folder in her hands. "Hi, my name is Charlene Booker, a Domestic Violence advocate assigned to your case. I was standing at the door. I heard everything you said, that was beautiful. I read a little about you in your file. Do you have anything else you would like to add?"

"Nope, not a thing. I'm tired of talking. I just think it's time for some action. I want to be released from here, go home, get my son, grab my things, and leave. I have nowhere to go, but I don't want to stay there."

"I never knew you had a son."

"Yes, I have a son, but he spends as much time upstairs as he can with his friends, so he won't see the shit that I have to go through."

"How old is he?"

"He is five. He is all I have. He already

saw his father beat my ass. I left that only to come here and deal with the same shit."

"Well, we have a shelter that has room for one more woman and her child, so you would make it even. They have room for 16 women and right now they are at 15. We can place you right away. Would you like that?" she asked.

"Yes, wherever I go, I hope he can't find me."

"Well, we will escort you to the house to grab your things."

"What if he is there?" I asked.

"We have a team of officers with us. I doubt he will try anything once we are there."

"Yeah, the same team of officers who keep defending him and calling me crazy, right?"

"Have a seat. I'll be back. Let me get your discharge papers and call over to the shelter to get them prepared for you."

Officer Tavi and Officer Lewis were still outside my room, roaming around, exchanging notes with the officers for the next shift.

Mrs. Booker came back in my room looking puzzled.

"What's wrong now?" I asked.

"Mrs. Thomas, what I am trying to figure out is how your husband is so cool at work and then abuses you at home? He has no record or any problems at work. He has never been written up in the four years he's been on the police force, unless he was tardy or called out sick or had a court date. The only reports I have are you filing them on him."

"Have you heard of Dr Jekyll and Mr. Hyde? That's him. Four years, he has not been written up because whatever happens at work, I get the suffering behind it. That damn revolver he brings home, he has threatened to blow my brains out if I say anything. He put the gun in my mouth and raped me. He took it from me. I didn't want to die, so I laid there with the gun in my mouth while he was raping me. He keeps reminding me he is a cop. He knows he can kill me and get away with it. He is fucking bipolar," I shouted. "Every time he comes home, it's me he takes it out on. What part don't you get?"

Officer Tavi kept watching me as I started walking around. "Yup, take a good look at me, because if you don't see me again, check for me in the morgue." I directed that statement to both of them sitting there looking at me. "Y'all need to stop protecting him. What exactly are you waiting for? Does he have to kill me and then you will take me seriously? He already kicked the baby out of my stomach, he already ruptured my ear, and he already put me in the hospital six times in one year. You forgot when he beat me so bad, and you came to the scene

STOP

and shook your head, I ended up in the hospital? What else does he have to do so y'all can lock him up? I hate him."

"Would you please sit down, Miss Thomas?"

"Nope, I don't want to sit down. I want to stand up. Why don't you sit down? I want to talk; I want you to listen. I want to get my point across. I hate being ignored."

He looked at me like I was crazy.

Mrs. Booker kept shaking her head. "Okay, as I was saying, after making some phone calls, this is what we figured out. The problem is you had a restraining order, but you did not go to court to extend it, so it was expired. Now we can extend it for 30 days as an emergency, but you will have to go to court if you want it continued. If not, in 30 days it will be expired. The choice is yours. We also have a car outside waiting for you. I will escort you to the house, allow you to go in and get your things."

"Listen, woman, how many times do I have to explain to you and your staff about the restraining order? Do you know how it works? Don't you know the moment he sees that; it will trigger him to harm me more? I am not going to keep explaining it again, because if y'all work for the law enforcement then you all will know you can't have a restraining order living in the same house with the abuser. The only way it will work is if I file it now and leave and go wherever you are taking me. If he happens to see me then he will be arrested because he is violating a restraining order. Please just drive me to the house so I can get this day over with. I'm exhausted. I've been up since 6:00 am, it's already 2:00 pm."

We got my discharge papers and headed to the car, driving to the house. I was not sure what to expect since I left early this morning. We parked in the parking lot. I got out of the car and walked up the stairs to the 2nd floor. One officer walked behind me, and two police officers stayed downstairs in case I needed protection. My neighbors were looking, trying to figure out what was going on, and why I was walking with an officer. I heard a lot of bickering and gossiping, but I didn't talk. I ignored them just like they ignored me when he was beating my ass. Shit, they never wanted to help when he was trying to kill me and throw me over the railing.

A few of his boys were downstairs. They were always there; it's all they do all day, every day, hang on the block and smoke weed. My son was on the 4th floor, looking down. He knew something wasn't right. He ran downstairs.

I said, "Come on, babes, we got to go," as I rushed him in the house.

"Wait, Mommy, can I tell my friends bye?"

"Sorry, no, we don't have much time. We have to leave right away."

I opened the door. I had a weird feeling James was in the house. My stomach tightened. I smelled death in the air. As I moved the curtain that separated our bedroom from the living room, I took a deep breath. Whew, thank God he was not home. I went in our room, put a towel on the bed with clothes, as if I was going to take a shower. I grabbed my little "already prepared" backpack and threw it over the fire escape. I went out the front door, holding my son, and met with the officers who were waiting for me. I went around the back, grabbed my bag, and got in the unmarked car. The officers drove behind us until we were out of the area, then they continued on to their destination. I bet you anything someone called James and told him what was going on. They love the drama.

My son started to ask a bunch of questions: "Mommy, where are we going? Mommy, why are you crying?" as he was wiping my face.

"Baby, I will explain later. Mommy is taking you somewhere where we will both be safe."

"Will I find new friends there?" he asked.

"I don't know. I hope so." Children are so innocent. All he wanted to do was be a child, and he had to be thrown into this mess. While looking out the window I was just thanking God for getting me out of this situation safe. No more pain, no more hurt, no more beatings, no more, no more, no more. I wiped my face from the tears. I'm sure that was the longest ride ever. I don't know where James was, but I wasn't waiting around to find out.

Charlene wanted to talk and ask questions on our ride to the house, but I got tired of talking about the same thing all the time. I just wanted to clear my thoughts. An hour later we pulled up to a nice big house in the middle of nowhere. We took so many turns, I didn't think I would know how to get back out if I wanted to. Thank you, Lord, we made it to our destination. We came out of the car. I walked up and waited for Charlene to do the introductions. She gave them my paperwork and highlighted it "Red flag," meaning I had an active restraining order. No one was allowed to call or come and get any information about me and my son.

For once I wasn't scared. I felt relaxed. I was shown to my room with a big queen size bed. I fell on the bed and looked up to the ceiling. Yes, all mine.

STOP

My son came over and lay on my chest. I hugged him so tight. I got up and put my Bible on the dresser and threw my little bag in the corner. I had nothing to unpack. I knew eventually I would have to talk with my son. He was young, so I had to be careful of the kind of words I said to him so he would understand, but not scare or confuse him. Glad this place has a 24-hour daycare. One of the ladies came and took him to meet and greet the other kids so I could get myself together.

I sat on my bed and read the rules, what to expect, and what not expect, all ten pages. I felt glad they didn't have an address. If I needed to get out, I had to call my advocate in advance, and she would make arrangements to come get me.

I received my care package like deodorant, toothbrush, toothpaste, towel and soap. They give you three months to get yourself together, and that was fine with me. I didn't even second guess what happened to James while I was gone as long as I was away from him. I had a long, stressful, painful, agonizing and depressing day, so I wanted to shower and sleep. We have a new member meeting tomorrow afternoon, so I'll meet the rest of the ladies then. I went to get my son to get him ready for bed. We both just lay there peacefully. We both slept right through the night.

I woke up late, which was awesome. That meant I slept well. Usually, when I was at home, I was up early in the morning because James had to find something to argue about or woke me up for painful sex.

We had a 10:00 meeting; just what I expected, the do's and don'ts. Don't let anyone give us a ride there.

Two days here, and I love it. I can actually focus.

We all had responsibilities and chores to do. Every day, a different person had a chore. We spent all morning, one-on-one with my counselor, writing up my three-months action plan, what I want now, my lifelong goals. Staying there was not an option for me, so I was not trying to sign my son up for school. I was trying to figure out my escape.

It was dinner time, so we all sat down and had dinner. I think someone gave them the memo that I loved chicken ziti and broccoli with Alfredo sauce, because that's exactly what we had. The house had sixteen ladies who were going through the same shit from our stupid boyfriends or husbands. A few had kids, a few didn't. We prayed over the food and started eating. I felt like a complete family.

The seating was organized with eight ladies on one side, eight on the other. Two house mothers were on each end. Listening to some of these women's stories, I wondered how they made it out alive.

    I was sitting at the table eating and staring into space.

    One of the ladies noticed a car coming in the driveway. A few of them looked outside. I wasn't expecting anyone, so I didn't look around. Well, my back was facing the window so I couldn't see outside anyway. The car left. Maybe the person wanted to turn around and head back out. A few minutes later, the same car came back up and reversed in the driveway again. No one comes here unless it's a personal pick up through the court system, or it's a new member, but I knew I was the last one to make the 16th member. Oh well, the car disappeared.

    We finished eating, cleaned up the kitchen, and went in the living room, getting to know each other. Conversing and laughing, just deciding what we are going to do when we leave there. One of the members told me another member got kicked out because she left here and went back with her ex-boyfriend to pick up her things, so I guess he convinced her to take him back. She was told to leave the house and her things will be mailed to her. They had to change all the locks in the place. You never know if he had a copy of the keys. They really protect you here. I heard so many stories, I was like wow.

An hour later, the same car drove in and pulled into the driveway. I thought it was a new member. When I looked closer, it was him. "Yup, that fucking bastard," I said under my breath. I looked around, not sure if anyone heard me.

Never in a million years would I say it was James. I saw the car and said, "You got to be kidding me." I didn't want to make a scene or alarm anyone.

I'm assuming after I left the house, he was waiting in the bushes for the officers to leave and followed us. I never looked back to see if anyone was following us and there were no suspicious lights behind us. He has done some secretive things in the past, so nothing he does surprises me.

When someone wants you dead, they will do anything they have to do to make that happen. Well, he will have to stay outside because I'm not getting kicked out of this shelter. I'm not even here a week yet. I snuck in the office and said, "Please call the police, my husband is outside. Please send them in an unmarked car because if he hears the sirens he will try to escape. I hope he doesn't show his ass. He wants me dead. He doesn't need to hurt the innocent ladies in here, they have been through enough."

James actually had the audacity to take God out his thoughts and walk up to the front door of the shelter. I don't know what he was thinking, or maybe he wasn't. In less than five minutes, three unmarked cars drove up on him. They exited the cars, drew their guns, and ordered him to put his hands up and walk backwards. He cooperated, put his hands on his head, and followed their instructions. We all just looked outside, shaking our heads while he was being led away into the police car. Another officer came up to the door so I could fill out a report. I already knew it was for me, so I went to meet him halfway.

The moment he entered my name in the system, he saw over 30 recent reports. He looked at me and shook his head. He said, "This dude is dangerous."

"Oh, you just figured that out?" I asked. "I've been trying to tell y'all that for the longest, but he is an officer with another district, and I can tell you all look out for each other, but he is still abusing his wife. I am sorry it had to take this for y'all to take me seriously. I thank God he did not hurt anyone here."

I apologized to the ladies and the staff. I already got a verbal warning; I ended up getting a written warning. It's fine. His foolishness was way beyond my control, but it was a safety issue. He was arrested and booked. I went to court the following week. I was escorted by my Advocate and two officers from the police department in a different district. I went just to make sure he goes down for this one.

    James was sentenced to jail for eight years, two years for each charge. He had a warrant for his arrest, violating a restraining order, causing bodily harm on his wife, and trespassing on private property. That's one less problem I have to worry about. Now that he is away, I can walk the streets with my head held high. He can't do anything to me. I just want to better myself.

    My son and I left after a month. We were placed in a safe house. They gave us a stipend of $500.00 each to travel and do what we had to do. I didn't want to do anything more but leave; being in the same country as that animal was mind boggling. I felt if I stayed there, he would have found me and would do something to me. Now that I knew he was in jail I went back to my old area where we both lived. I filled them in on everything that happened. One of the neighbors said that is how he is to everyone, he is a very ignorant man, he snaps at everyone and everything. They knew not to intervene when he was abusing me; he would have flipped out on them. I told them: Never stand there and watch a man hitting any woman and keep quiet; they could have saved me from all this mess. One tenant told me she prayed for me every night. She heard my screams, she heard my cries, she heard the fights. She has a daughter and she can't imagine a man putting his hands on her daughter. I asked her why she never said something. Another lady told me he just had a baby with another woman. I heard so many stories about him.

I made it to the internet café, searched for some shelters, and booked a flight out of the country. I found myself back in the US. We stayed in a shelter and got help with our own apartment. I've had a few bumps in the road, but I survived. Every now and then, I flinch when I hear a siren or see an officer, but I'll get over it. I did call and thank Officer Tavi, Officer Carnegie, and Officer Lewis for doing the best they could have done. I understand their hands were tied and their choices were limited.

I also sent a card to Miss Booker, giving her an update on my life.

I'm on my way to starting my life.

I did have that talk with my son about what happened and why we left. As he gets older, he still asks about him. I still have the same answer. He is out of the picture. I wrote a book about all that I have been through with him and just other things in life I've experienced. I'm working on three more books. It's a lot of stories about hope, love, and inspiration. I now teach women to watch out for the signs and how to escape a Domestic Violence relationship. I am determined to make my painful life experience a lesson to women out there who need advice, love, support, courage, strength and hope. Sometimes I pick up my book, look at it, front and back, and say, "Wow, I did this." I'm changing lives. One page at a time.

I DO (JANUARY 24, 2009)

Finally, the day and the time has arrived for me to say, "I do" or, as they say, to spend my last day single. After months of planning, everything was in place, a little closer to perfection. The limo arrived at the church. I stepped out in style, walked into the church, with the choir singing in the background. The photographer was busy taking pictures. I just found out I was pregnant. It was a beautiful day – the day that every woman looks forward to. Well, at least, that is what I thought.

My fiancé came from a tight-knit, church-going family. They were very close; he was always with them, at least when I was there, unless it is all a perfect act. They knew about me for four years while we were engaged. When I was with them (before we married), I was the only one for them; I was the best daughter-in-law in the world.

During the engagement, we had no problems, no disrespect. He never had any females in my face, so there was nothing to discuss. I am now looking at it like, he probably told them not to come around when I'm there. I wasn't sure how he worked that out, but he was good.

The day I got married, I jokingly said to myself that when the pastor asked, "Does anyone have anything to say on why this couple should not get married, speak now or forever hold their peace," I expected someone to say something. This man was too good to be true. I know nothing in life is perfect, but he took the cake; however no one said anything. The minute the pastor pronounced us husband and wife, and we were walking out of the church, he gripped my hand tightly. I paid it no attention, but I know now it was the first sign: he started controlling me immediately after the wedding.

When we went to take pictures, he was telling me how to pose, who to smile with, what to do and what not to do. I was a little alarmed. We made it to the reception. I spent more time being pulled away to hear different people tell me different stories. A few women he was sleeping with came to the reception. I'm not sure why, maybe they wanted to know who I was. Or to let me know they were sleeping with him and was not going to stop. I was very uncomfortable. It was really too much to take in all at once. Again, he started controlling me right away, telling me how to dance, who to dance with, and what to eat. We had a little misunderstanding because I got tired of the embarrassment where he was talking down on me and making me feel like I was nothing in front of all his friends and family.

Within 24 hours, now that the ring was on my finger and the title was now "Husband and Wife," people were coming out of everywhere with a story to tell; they were all desperate to tell me something about him. But I had been there all the time and they never said anything to me. Day by day, hint by hint, one clue after another, it all started coming to light. He spent more time with his friends on our wedding day than he did with me. I knew something was wrong with that picture.

The man of my dreams went from having no kids to having two women pregnant while we were walking down the aisle. Again, going back to what I said about their family being close-knit: Someone in that family knew something. They say "only a mother knows," well the family knew but didn't want to lose me as a daughter-in-law, so they had to keep it a secret. They had to keep the women away.

After I cried and was shocked, hurt, and angry, I asked him why. "Why did you do this to me? How could you cheat on me?"

He told me God wanted him to have a

baby.

"Wait, what? God wanted you to have a baby with the woman you married, not just any chick."

Now that he had a child with her, he felt like it was a privilege to continue having sex with her. He told me I am the wife so he could say he has a wife, and she is the baby's mother for a reason, and we are all going to hell anyway. Keep in mind this man was in church every single Sunday and at every event the church had. It makes me wonder what kind of God he was really serving. But you know what? I realized he was only going to church when I was there to make me feel like he is really a godly man.

Seeing that he had a one-track mind and was not the best person to talk to, I went to the pastor of the church where we were both members. I told him what was on my mind. The pastor decided to over-talk me and tell me that I needed to learn how to adapt to being married and I needed to be submissive to my husband. He gave me a word to concentrate on. The word was "PREPARE." He told me that I need to prepare for things, so when it happens, it wouldn't hurt as much. He threw me off, because he was not listening to what I had to say. He said what he wanted to say and the problem was never solved. I had to get my point across, but his whole point was that it's not even a month yet, and I am already complaining. In this religion you can only marry once. If I was to get a divorce, God will be mad at me. I was thinking, "What? Nah ... there is no way in this world a man can be treating me like this and you are telling *me* I can't get a divorce." Maybe this is in your religion, but the God that I serve does not want any fools in his kingdom. Too many marriages end up in divorce and I don't think God will be mad at his people.

As the wife, I decided to visit this young woman who lives directly across the yard from where I live, this so-called friend/bridesmaid with no type of confrontation. Yes, the same one who helped me pick out the bouquet, the same one who decorated the tables for me at the reception. We sat in the same room and ate and talked together, and all this time she was pregnant with my husband's child, which was hard. I wanted to hear her side because we all know there are three sides to everyone's story, his side, her side, and then the truth, because I know they were both lying to me. I went to her house and had a talk. I listened to her side. We sat down. I allowed her to talk first.

She said, "Sis, listen!"

I looked around like, *Who you calling 'sis?'* My eyes opened wide. "Hold up, dear, it's not 'sis,' it's you and I here. Because if you were a real sister, it does not matter what he said or did, you should not open your legs to my man. You could have come and asked me but continue."

She said he told her we were not together anymore.

I said, "Listen, chick, a man will tell you anything to get in your drawers. We have been together for four years. You may not see me around because I travel a lot, but trust me, we are together."

She said yes, they had sex and when she told him she was pregnant, he told her to keep it a secret.

"Okay, young lady," I addressed her, "if we were not together, why were you helping me plan a wedding? Who the hell you thought I was marrying?" She got quiet because she got busted in a lie. "There is no need for you to defend him, but listen to me, the same thing he did to me he would do to you. Please don't think you are any more of a woman than me by doing what you did."

Now, I'm not stupid. I knew she was pregnant, just never knew it was by him. I got the answers I was looking for; it may not be what I wanted to hear, but I got my answers. My next move was to get out, because this was way too early in the marriage, and I know with a baby involved, he would have to be in her life for a lifetime. We had been engaged for three years, I just moved here in December, we got married in January, and filing for divorce in March; this was not in my plans.

He was mad that I confronted his outside woman. I walked back in the house. He asked me why I had to question her. I said, "Well, you are not saying anything, so why not?"

He put his hands around my neck to choke me. His mom and sister were there, but he got to me quickly enough to throw me to the floor. I desperately tried to stop him from kicking me – I covered my eyes, mouth and stomach to protect myself, but to no avail. He savagely attacked me with his construction boots. Everywhere I tried to protect was hit anyway. After I got up, I realized I was bleeding.

"So, wait, you cheated on me, but you are mad at me, right?" I asked him.

"It was not your place to ask her," he shouted.

Yeah okay, dude, whatever. "So, you'd rather protect your other woman than your wife?" I asked him. I looked down and noticed I was bleeding.

He pointed at me and said, "Yo, you are bleeding. You need to go to the hospital."

Well duh! I know I do! Anyway, I went to the bathroom to clean up and change my clothes, trying to stay strong through the tears. I knew he caused me to have a miscarriage, but he never knew I was pregnant. I had no time to tell him. We went straight to the wedding, to the reception, to home, to blows. I headed out the door with him to the car, to go to the hospital. He kept talking to me through my tears, asking me what I was going to tell them. He was actually giving me choices of what I could and could not say!

I said, "No, I will tell them I just got married and you are putting your hands on me. I will tell them what you did."

He gave me a guilt trip, saying that he will get locked up. I said, "You should've thought about that before you put your hands on me." So, I walked out the door with him. How nice of the abuser to walk his battered wife to the hospital. He is the first person they would question.

Anyway, I went down the stairs, and as I was about to get in the car to head out to the hospital, he still tried to talk me out of going, telling me the hospitals are packed and since I'm not from the Island, they will not want to take the risk of seeing me. Every excuse he could think of, he tried. I finally gave in and said, "I got this." I went upstairs and went to sleep.

Seeing that the family was blind, he (the husband) was not wrapped too tight, and the pastor was on a different page, I said the next best thing was to escape. I just put on my actor's hat and acted like I was happy, pretending everything was alright. I woke up the next morning, I cleaned the whole room, and packed up my bags. I didn't take everything; any casual observer would think I had only cleaned the room. The following day, he went to work and called to ask me how my day was going. "Great," I said. He had no idea I was already in a car to the airport. His next call was to ask if I wanted him to bring me lunch. I told him exactly what I wanted to eat, but I was already checking in and boarding my flight. So, he thought he was going to keep abusing me and treating me like a dog? Nope! He was wrong. By the time he got home to bring me the food, I was on a plane back to Boston. When I got there, I went to the hospital and realized that his constant physical abuse and stress caused me to lose my child. I wanted to surprise him and tell him after the wedding that I was pregnant, but I was more surprised by his secretive actions.

Many may ask why I did not leave sooner. Keep in mind that I had no family where I was. I gave up everything I had in Boston. I sold my house to be with this monster. Where was I going to escape to? I noticed a lot of men like to get married and move far with their wives so when they are doing dirt, the women have no way out. So, they can have that constant control over them.

After a few months back, I collected my thoughts, picked up the pieces of my heart, glued them back together, filed for divorce, and kept on moving. Everyone was telling me I need to get over it because it already happened. I did that, but why lead someone on? Why plan a big wedding? Why go all out and you damn well know you had two women pregnant the day you were saying "I DO?" I looked and felt like a complete jackass.

My heartfelt message to the ladies: Please don't get married to make your family happy, or for the kids, or just to have a title. If it is not for love, trust and honest communication, then forget it. It's easy to get married, but the divorce is devastating.

STOP

AS I LEAVE YOU

You and I would drive around for hours
or take romantic walks,
Hand in hand through the park,
having serious talks
About how happy you are
that I am in your life
And in years to come
you would make me your wife.
All the cards you bought me
proved your love
Phone calls proved
I was the one you were thinking of.
There was nothing in this world
I wouldn't have done for you
Now you forced me to make a decision
so I'm leaving you
I did things for you
I never did for anyone else
At one time I loved you more than life itself
We used to laugh, play,
and joke with each other
We used to share secrets to be better lovers
I loved you in ways
I couldn't possibly love anyone else
I wrote you many letters and poems
on how you were treating me
But you were in too deep or too blind to see

*You became very controlling
and very demanding
Very insecure and not understanding
You saw the signs coming,
you just couldn't believe
That after all these years
I would get up and leave.
I know I did my best;
you think you'd understand
That I never had a problem knowing
how to treat my man.
I know there are a lot of fish in the sea,
So why were you stuck on this fish?
I mean ME?
I invested weeks, months and some years
Now you've got me drowning in tears
I would rather be alone and happy
Than to be with you and feel crappy
Yeah, it hurts that it came to an end
But I don't want to be your lover,
not even your friend
This was not something I planned to do,
But I thought I'd let you know why I left you
We are no longer a couple
but at times I sit here and cry
From the emotional, physical and verbal
abuse that you still deny.
Now you can go your way and I will go mine
Don't even worry about me; I will be fine.
I did everything for us;
I worked two jobs to keep us going
But you had other relationships
without me knowing
See, all the years I held you down*

STOP

I didn't know you were playing around
You had women's pictures lying around
Numbers in your pocket
and you just kept on lying
But me being me,
I still believed and kept trying.
You left for days,
you turned your cell phone off.
Like it has been said, I am too soft.
I took you back;
thought I was doing the right thing
I just kept opening my door and heart
and letting you back in
Females calling the house asking for you
Now tell me, what was I supposed to do?
Believe me boo;
there will be no tears shed over you.
I thought we would have made a difference
in each other's life
This is hurting
more than a sharp-jagged knife.
I was warned about men like you
See what I get? I thought I was grown.
I learned the hard way;
I found out on my own.
I can go on and on till thy kingdom come,
But why will it matter?
The damage is already done.
You made it possible
for the next man to love me
And treat me right;
things you did not do, he did.
Places you could not take me, he did.
Thank you for leaving me.

Thank you for allowing me to spread my wings and fly.

When I had the courage and the strength to escape, I did.

My first attempt to escape failed. I told a close friend what you were doing; they said it was me and I needed to get used to being married to you. You jumped up one morning and just started swinging; I guess it was me again – huh? Or were you just tripping? I knew when I left, I was not coming back.

In front of friends and family, you were all smiles, deeply in love, but when they were gone, "hmmm," it was easier for you to push and shove. When I got on the plane, I said: "Thank you, Lord; not me, again." My escape was me saving my life so I could be someone else's wife. You see, men like you make it harder for women like me to trust again.

God put me through this because he had a better plan. Women who have been abused always say "why me?" But I am living proof to let you know it is not you or us; we are not in control and we should not blame ourselves for anything. I learned it is a cycle that needs to be broken; all men are not the same. I had some time to think and I realized that I don't need you. I realized I loved you and you liked me. I wanted you and you cared for me. My feelings were stronger for you than you can imagine. You were my soulmate, the love of my life, my friend, my husband. We stood in front of the church and made a vow to God. I kept mines, you didn't.

I can breathe now. I don't have to have butterflies in my stomach anymore. I am over you; now you can go. Keep it moving and make someone else miserable. No more wondering about how you feel about me; it's irrelevant.

The first day I met you, I was happy that I found you.

Now, I am even happier I don't have to be around you.

Who cares now; I am over you.

Now I am not bitter or blue.

Believe it is true,

All that love I wasted for you,

It no longer matters.

My heart used to go pitter-patter.

I felt like I was on top of the world, but those were my own feelings; you had none. You didn't care about my feelings. I am over you. You would never believe it if I said not too long ago how much I loved you. So now I look deep inside myself enough to simply let you go. Bye. I am happy! I am over you and I feel unleashed like a lion released into the jungle, running free and not trapped in a small, little den. Hands open wide, telling the world, "I'm free! I'm free!" I am over you. I know I am over you, really I am…but I remind myself that all I was to you was a game. I loved you, I really did!

I know I don't love you;
I know that for a fact,
'Cause now I know that this was all an act.
I know better than to love someone
who won't love me back.
I know I am over you, and that is the truth….
Because my heart no longer belongs to you!
When we first met and we talked,
you said three things you don't like:
A liar, embarrassment and disrespect.
Well, you must really hate yourself;
that is all I got from you.
At times I thought I was out of my mind,
Thinking a real man, I would never find.
See you cluttered my innocent mind,
Or as they would say "love is blind."
When you left for work
I said this is my chance to run.
I caught you in lies but did not want to argue,
so I accepted it and just kept quiet,
'Cause when I tried to talk to you,
it turned into a riot.
I never prepared for my life
to turn out like this.
It started simply with a kiss.
While I was walking down the aisle
preparing to say, "I do,"

STOP

*You had your mind made up
with what you wanted to do.
I knew at the wedding, people were saying,
"What an ass."
See, they knew about your present,
not to mention your past.
You had a plan when you took my hand.
Didn't know so soon
that it was going to hit the fan.
You played the game;
you got what you wanted.
Never knew your past was so haunted.
Yes, I asked and I checked out the scenery
before I said "I do,"
But sometimes people are just very good
at what they do.
You played me good for four years straight.
I guess I found out about you a little too late.
If I found out before I said "I do,"
I would have never married you.
People said long-distance love affairs
never work,
I tried to prove them wrong,
now I look like a jerk.
I can't lie;
I am hurt at what you have done,
And I am the one left
to explain this to my son.
I have to teach him while he is young,
you see,
Because I don't want him to do to women
what you did to me.
Don't say yes when you meant to say no.
Don't stay if you wanted to go.*

*One of the reasons I did not stay
I did not want my son to think it was okay.
You see, some women fight back
and some of us don't.
Some will get to read this and some won't.
Remember when we met?
You told me everything
that you wanted me to know.
From the time we spent together,
we couldn't let each other go.
You said I was everything
you were looking for.
We spent hours at a time
on the phone and even more.
We took trips to see each other;
we had so much fun.
The act you put on,
I never thought we would be done.
I thought you were the one – you were
like no other.
I thought you were the last one
when I introduced you to my mother.
You did a 360;
you just flipped and changed.
My hopes, dreams,
and future plans you tried to rearrange.
You did exactly what you said
you were not going to do.
You left me all screwed up.
I still don't believe you!
I saw you today
and I went home and cried.
No, I am not missing you,
really this is why.*

I cried to see how you can hurt me and move on with your life like nothing happened. While I am left to heal from a battered body, broken heart and shattered dreams, clearly you have moved on – trust me; same here. When I saw you, I jumped; not that I am scared of you, but.... all the bad memories came to my mind again. I don't cry over you; I cry for the next woman that ends up with you.

Reminiscing...I must say I have been involved in some hurtful relationships. People say I allow myself to get hurt, but no one likes to get hurt. When you are in love, you want it to work and you do your best to make it work, but... it takes two. You get tired of being alone. And you feel the next man will treat you better, but he was just as bad as the one you just left. Everyone is not the same and everybody deserves a chance, but, remember, some men don't even love themselves. How they can love you?

A MESSAGE TO THE LADIES

To all my beautiful sisters and women: I see what you go through. Remember, I am one. I am speaking as a single mother who is raising a son. First and foremost, ladies, you must love yourself before you can love anyone else. Love is within you. We are called "women" for a reason. We need to be better than what we are settling for. Please stop dealing with men who don't see the beauty in you. You say all these men are telling you the same thing. Why do you think they are telling you this?

Why do they want to be with you? You say you are tired and they don't respect you. They want what they can get from you, and if anyone comes and occupies that space they feel is theirs, then there's a problem.... The way I see it, these men don't want you because you are a single parent, working, strong, independent, beautiful, educated and smart.... they are overlooking all of that.

There is more to us than what they are seeing. You need to start dealing with men who know the inner you and don't want to have you for just one night..... Remember, no man can love you based on your body.... If that's all they care about, then stop dealing with them. Don't tell me you don't know when a man is just interested in one thing.... Have some respect for yourself and stop dealing with men who are Unworthy of you. If a man doesn't love you, if you have to force him to be with/spend time with you, if you have to keep calling him or leaving messages and he ignores your calls, he is not worth it. A man will only treat you the way you allow him to treat you. You fall in love with them and they break your heart.... What do you do when he breaks your heart?

Don't think of it as the end; think of it as a brand-new start.

Don't let him see you fall apart. Don't make him feel like you are nothing without him. Your ex is your ex. Your past is your past. Nothing in life is supposed to last.

*Ladies, a man can only get
what you give him.
If a man wants you,
nothing can keep him away.
And if he doesn't want you,
nothing can make him stay.
Relationships were not meant to be easy;
I know you get tired and fed up.*

*It was just a stepping stone, so stay strong,
move on, and keep your head up.
Don't ever let a man feel
that he won in his game.
Part of loving someone
is learning to let go.
Believe me; I've been there,
so I should know.
Don't give up on hope;
just letting you know.
If you present yourself as a gift,
he will work harder for the prize.
Ladies, stop making it so easy for him
to get between your thighs.*

A LETTER TO THE LADIES

    I am asking you to pay close attention to the next few poems; I dedicate them to you. Don't ever say or think it won't happen. It could happen to you or someone you know. I think it is time to take things very seriously. I keep hearing about husbands killing wives or wives killing husbands. There has to be some kind of sign in the relationship telling you to get out. Life is too short to be playing games, especially if you have kids involved. I am not the smartest female in the world, but a man only has to show me one sign and I am out of there. There is not enough love in the world for me to get shot, stabbed, beaten or killed.

<u>A speech I gave at a battered women's shelter</u> *(location withheld):*

    There is a song called "We Fall Down (But We Get Up." And it reminds me why we are here today. I am sure many of us were down, and while we were there, we were not sure how we were going to get back up, but we did.

If I can wave a magic wand to put an end to domestic violence, then consider it waved. I came from being battered and broken to beautiful and blessed. Disappointed to anointed, I passed the test. I made the impossible possible. Never in a million years did I think I would have been a victim. I mean, from my son's father to my ex-husband to dating, abuse after abuse after abuse. The moment I got up and out of that relationship, I said God gave me a chance to live so I can teach others how I did it.

Looking at you, I see survivors; I see strong women; I see strength.

I am not sure what happened, why you are here, but someone had to push you to this point. I am so glad you decided that enough was enough and you did something about it. Some women were not so lucky. They are either dead or lying in the hospital bed recovering from their scars, burns, black eyes, and bruises. Your time here is not to be bitter, but to be better. This is your time to heal; take as much time as you need to find yourself. Prepare yourself mentally not to allow yourself to be in another domestic-violence relationship. Of course, we never know when it's going to happen, but be on guard.

If you leave here with anything today,

leave knowing that you were courageous and you loved yourself enough to make a change, to put an end to the situation. You can teach others not to make the same mistake you made or how to prevent it from happening.

Me, on the other hand, I thought about killing my abusers, but I knew I had a son to raise, so I just walked away. Notice, I said "abusers," 'cause I had more than one.

My first abuse was sexual, at age nine. I thought it was normal, until I told someone. That ended when I was 13; then it was on again. This time, it was someone who clearly did not want me. She told me numerous stories about how hard she tried to abort me. After years of insult, disrespect, lies, neglect, I'd had enough of that, left, got married; talk about jumping straight into the fire! It only got worse – physical, embarrassment, cheating. The last time he put his hands on me was the last time he put his hands on me. The moment I found myself on the ground, covering my stomach and face from his blows, I said nah, I have been to too many funerals, made too many hospital visits reaching out to women who have been in a DV relationships. Too many women were looking up to me.

A lot of people say some women allow it to happen; I agree to a point. Some women allow it by going back or taking back their abusers, but you must remember others that can't escape. Some of us gave up our families to be with these monsters and have no way out... their abuser is all they have. They make them feel like no one else will want them... I was one; I did not allow it, but I put an end to it.

    To be loved is a great feeling and we all want to love and or be loved by someone, but if you don't love yourself first, how can you learn to love someone else? I was able to love again after years of abuse, because I let him know my expectations and I raised my standards.

STOP

BUT I LOVE HIM

What will it take for you to leave this guy?
Does he have to give you another black eye?
He does not love you if he spits on you.
He is not a man if he hits on you.
He calls you names and causes you to hurt.
All he does is treat you like dirt.
You tell me one good thing about this man.
Don't tell me you love him,
because he doesn't give a damn.
He does not want you to
call your friends on the phone.
He does not trust you with others or alone.
When he hits you, he says, "I love you."
Oh, what a lie.
Remember: Love does not come
with a black eye.
To be in love, it has to be shared.
Love does not mean you have to be scared.
If this man continues
to do these things to you
And you are still with him,
then I am sorry for you.
The truth... can you handle it?

Broken bones, makeup to cover up the scars, sunglasses when there is no sun. How many more beatings, black eyes, bruises, hospital visits do you have to go through before you get out of this relationship? Every time you turn around, a woman is being battered. You can prevent it from happening to you. When you see the first controlling, insecure sign, or clue, get out/get help. I don't want to hear that he only hit you once. That is enough! Talk to a friend or a family member. Once is a mistake, twice is a habit, three times you are overdoing it. Hit me once, shame on you... Hit me twice, shame on me.

You know, we sometimes get ourselves into relationships and think we are in love and we can never find anyone else. All the excuses about the kids and the marriage, but behind closed doors we are getting our asses kicked. He does not love you if he is actually hitting you, knocking you down to the floor, punching, slapping, and kicking, choking, biting, even using deadly force. And you are still telling me you love him? Oh, you need to wake up!

Ladies, don't feel that in order to be loved, you need to be hit. *Baby, I love you;* but later, he is whipping your ass. Ladies, stop finding excuses for these men. Don't waste your time on no user, no loser, and no abuser. If he can't respect you, he needs to be left alone.

Ladies, why do you take out a restraining

order and then go back, mess with, or sleep with the same man? A restraining order is an order of protection, meaning you stay away from him and he stays away from you. If he hides in the closet, goes through your room, checks your phone caller ID, calls your job, your parents, and questions everybody about you, that is not love – that is control. Ladies, when your body ends up in a drain or in a wheelchair, it will be too late for an explanation.

There is a reason why they are called EX-boyfriends. I am sick of seeing or hearing that a woman was killed by her ex-lover the week after she took out a restraining order. Ladies, if you keep provoking the situation, it will not work. If you continue to let a man put his hands on you, then you are exposing yourself to a world of trouble. Ladies, I stress the subject because it is no joke. Close your legs and open your eyes. Read the papers; listen to the news. See how many violent relationships turn deadly. I will continue talking about this subject until the day I die. Tears come to my eyes when I have to sit here and beg women to protect themselves. Yes, we all need to be loved, but if you don't love yourself, you can't love anybody else. You have to live for YOU. Your life is worth more than that. He will tell you he is sorry; he won't do it again; there you go again giving him another chance. If you stay, you may not get a second chance.

There's a big difference between wanting a man and needing a man. Ladies, you figure it out: There is no excuse for abuse. Fear isn't love. You lie, you find all the excuses, you always have an alibi for him. He beat your ass, you call the police; when the police take him, you cry when they lock him up, and you go visit him. He gets out; he does it again. Really, what is going through your head? You pretend to be the perfect couple, but behind closed doors you are not sure you will live to see tomorrow. There is nothing you can possibly tell me or no reason why you stay, because I really don't want to hear it anyway.

In case you didn't know, domestic violence is not just among women. Men are also abused by their partners. Do you know how many men are abused each year by their partners? A lot!

Domestic violence is so tragic and painful. It can and will take a toll on you. Let's just put a STOP to this! Always remember – treat people the way you want them to treat you. There is help. You can reach out and you will be helped.

STOP

I LOVE U, I HATE U {pick one}

You say you love me,
but you hit me.
The same eyes that you looked into
are now black and blue.
When you were hitting me
I looked at you in your eyes,
You were so angry because
I caught you in more lies.
You lied and cheated on me;
what am I worth if there is infidelity?
I told you how I felt;
one blow to my face was what I was dealt.
You got upset at me
when I tried to fight back.
You would hit me harder – Flashbacks.
Memories,
every song that plays on the radio
reminds me of you.

I look at all the talk shows and the court shows. I keep asking, "How can these women allow that? Oh, no man can ever do that to me. If that was me I would...." Yeah, right. I would do what? Not a darn thing ... because that was me. I have the pictures to prove it. I thank God that I left. Now you want to say you are sorry. You are right; that is exactly what you are – sorry, 'cause real men do not hit women. I am a delicate, beautiful woman; this pretty face is for you to look at, not hit and abuse.

I took a long ride and the tears were just flowing

People saw a different side of you; I played it off without anyone knowing.

Sorry, there was no way I could have kept this in any longer – I would have been dead by now. The reason why I have to say something is my cry for help can open another woman's eyes. What happened in your past, do not bring that to my future! I was the one that was standing up in front of crowds, talking to women about not allowing men to hit and abuse them. I was the one that was telling and talking to women about sexual abuse. How do you think I know? I have been through it. Again, "Who feels it, knows it."

STOP

IT HAPPENED AGAIN

So, I finally fell in love with this guy.
After all I been through in life,
I said all men are not the same;
let me give him a try.
He started out nice for a while,
but then I no longer saw that smile.
I saw the controlling signs;
I heard the anger in his voice.
He started coming in late,
doing what he wanted to do.
Leaving me in the house,
he was always on his way to take me out
and he never made it.
I sat by the window wondering,
"Is he really on his way?"
He never came. I came in one day
And as I opened the door,
He surprised me with one hit to the floor.
He violently dragged me in the room.
The last thing I heard was BOOM.
Ten minutes later, I felt strange.
I said, "What the heck?"
This idiot had his hands around my neck.
He was trying to kill me, not sure why.
I thought, "How can he say he loves me,
but wants me to die?"

He promised me he will never hit me
He would never do what the last man did.
Sad how you cheated; you left me,
And I have to feel the pain.
Not me, never again.
I am tired of you loving me with your fist.
This is not love, what is this?
Tired of looking for love
in all the wrong places,
I don't need my child
to see all these different faces.
You thought the flowers,
cards and apologies were going to work.
Well they didn't;
now don't you feel like a jerk?
My body got weak from all the blows.
You made me feel like a bird
with a broken wing.
"Helpless"
But this bird got up
and had to spread her wings and fly.
If I stayed in this relationship,
I would have died.
You wanted me, you got me;
you didn't know how to treat me.
You mistook me for a rug
because all you did was beat me.
I stayed a little while;
your behaviors I tried to rearrange
But how can I forget
"a penny has no change?"
I am a woman of strength and beauty.
Rule #1 – don't put your hands on me!
Too many women allow it and call it love.

STOP

How can they get that confused
with push-and-shove?
My hands no longer tied;
my heart is no longer heavy
from hate, anger and disgust.
You left me in a mess;
didn't know who to trust.
My lows turned into highs;
my NOs turned into YES
From bitter and broken
to beautiful and blessed,
I felt trapped, suffocated,
like I couldn't breathe
I knew I had to find a way to leave.
My broken wings
are now nurtured and healed.
I couldn't talk back then
because my lips were sealed.
The name-calling, verbal abuse
day in and out.
Intimacy forced,
you took it when you wanted it.
I never loved you;
just laid there and dealt with it.
Eyes closed, couldn't look you in your face.
I don't ever want another woman
to be in my place.
Bright smiles faked
when others came around.
People questioned why I was so quiet;
they didn't know I didn't want to start a riot.
Release, relieved that I am free;
don't want another woman to end up like me.
Feet unshackled,

free so I can walk, live, breathe.
Talk to other women
who are facing the same abuse.
I wanted to tell you how I felt; couldn't say
much with all the blows that was dealt.
The moment you choked me in front my son,
I threw my hands up and say I AM DONE!
See, you left me for dead,
but God had a better plan.
Not for me to be abused
by you or any other man.
He saw me struggling and gave me strength.
He knew you were a coward
and made me courageous.
He made the impossible possible.
See, I didn't lose my faith;
you didn't take my soul.
It's not my fault
you don't know how to play the husband role.
Maybe if I didn't answer back with a "what,"
my eyes wouldn't be closed shut.
Or maybe if I didn't disagree
and let you have your way,
we wouldn't be where we are today.
No, no; better yet,
if I allowed you to keep beating my ass,
I wouldn't be in my room,
hoping this day will pass.

WHEN WILL IT END?

*Another friend of mine got murdered by
someone she trusted.
Her body was found dismembered;
it got me disgusted.
She gave him her heart; he took her life.
Was this part of the vows
they took as husband and wife?
A man is supposed to love his woman;
a woman supposed to love her man.
But unfortunately, he had a different plan.
I wish someone had heard her cries;
I wish someone had told her
the marriage was all lies.
I wish I was there to wipe the tears
from her eyes.
This sick bastard stabbed her to death.
He stood over her body
till she took her last breath.
I warned her about men like him;
she said: "Empress, I'm fine."
She went her way; I went mine.
So why am I seeing this
on my Facebook timeline?
I'm mad, I'm frustrated,
and yes, I am hurting.
I knew that I really lost her*

when they closed the curtain...
You're probably wondering
why we are all gathered here
It's because people like you
did not want to interfere.
You knew what was going on,
but you choose not to help.
You can't blame anyone else but yourself.
You knew it all along
that he was beating her ass.
But you made no attempt to help
every time you passed.
You heard her screaming
while he held her mouth shut.
You heard her bawl
when he burned her with the cigarette butt.
You said it was not your business;
you refused to intervene.
Maybe you were scared
'cause he was so mean.
You chose to ignore the noise;
you said "Why bother?"
Fellas! Would you have let that happen
to your mother?
So, now do you know why
we are all gathered here?
Because this scene is something we fear.
So now that this poem has come to a close,
all I ask is if you can help, please impose...
Ashes to ashes, dust to dust...

SHE IS NO LONGER HERE

I came to see you this morning. I knocked on your door. You asked what I was here for. Again, I came to try and protect you; not trying to change you, but I am tired of hearing your cries. My walls are thin. I wish I could reach within and grab you away from him. I can't even sleep at night; I don't remember my dreams because my new alarm is your early-morning screams. Anger in his voice is all I hear. Every morning playing the waiting game to see who will call the police. The last time they came, you took the blame; you kept lying, I kept trying. I called because I thought you were dying. You told me it was not my business. You love him and no other man can take his place. Stop!!! Look in the mirror – did you see your face?

I came to see you today, this time in a hospital room, looking at the teddy bears, love balloons, and all the "I'm sorry" letters. Your face looks like a jigsaw puzzle. He hit you so hard it ruptured your ear, but you are telling me there is nothing to fear. All I was trying to do was protect you, my dear. I no longer want him to inject you with more blows and hits with balled-up fists; again, you told me to mind my business. So, I did, like a kid who did something wrong: "I hid."

A few months passed. I heard nothing. I'm so glad things got better; people do change. I was so wrong, that's why I am writing this letter. Now I came to see you again, only now you are lying down quietly. Beautiful coffin; this is where I tried to protect you from going, but this dude had you messed up without even knowing. I remembered you told me no other man can take his place. I am here now so another woman won't take your place. I only hope she listens to me.

STOP

I DANCE, I RISE, I DEMAND

*I dance because I can –
I dance for women, children and men
Everywhere – Knowing that we no longer
have to live in fear.
Together, we can all put an end
to domestic violence.
No longer do we have to stand in silence –
No more hands over my mouth!
No more being afraid!
No more daddy hitting mommy,
Children hiding in the corner,
Not knowing what will happen next –
All because of a text
You flip the script
And start to hit...
Man, enough of this ISH!
I don't regret the day we met but
I won't forget...
You thought I was your pet –
You can't take me to the vet!
It's over; my mind is set.
I dance to release my frustration.
To build a better generation –
No more negative penetration
in my mind...*

I rise
From the bottom to the top
'Cause my goal in life is to put a stop
To this
Body black-and-blue
Eyes swollen 'cause of you –
Ribs broken
No words are spoken.
I rise up from the hospital bed
Where you left me for dead
After beating me with a gun in the head
And you call THAT love?
Nah, dread!
I demand
A stop to physical
Verbal
Mental
Sexual
Abuse –
Not again, my friend…
Today is where it all ends.
I demand you stop playing games!
I demand you stop calling me names!
I demand you stop putting your hands on me!
I demand you start treating me
With equality…
I Dance!
I Rise!
I Demand!

STOP

HERE I STAND

*Here I stand in front of you
to say, "NO MORE."
No more will I take any more blows.
No more will he be allowed to break my nose.
I stand strong on my own two feet.
Don't want my past to be on repeat.
From this day on I'm taking back my life.
Did you know I was a battered wife?
Strong and independent is who I am.
That is why I am here; to take a stand.
Constant reminders of your abuse
blinded by love:
You slap, pull my hair and spit on me.
Made me cut my dreads
so no one would want me.
But I still stand strong;
won't let you bring me down.
Ladies, men – you don't have to stay.
There's no reason for anyone
to treat you that way!
You need to be loved,
but most of all, respected.
No one should make you feel neglected.*

*Are you willing to take a stand with me?
Don't let Domestic Violence
take you away from your family.*

COLLEEN WILLIAMS

NO LONGER BLACK AND BLUE

I saw you a year ago;
you started a new relationship.
I was so happy for you,
but then I started seeing less and less of you.
You were always busy;
we couldn't do the things
we used to do anymore.
Every time I called,
you had to hang up the phone.
You never told me what was
going on – that was your biggest mistake.
I found out while I was viewing
your body at your wake.
It's funny; when you first met him,
he took you out.
And showed you what being in love
was all about.
He told you he loved you;
you told him the same.
Then he started calling out your name.
As soon as he got you
wrapped under his wing.
Now he's started doing his own thing.
The first strike to your face,
he said he was sorry.
But you know he loves you

so, "why worry?"
The second strike caused your eyes
to be black-and-blue.
You had always thought
it won't happen to you.
The third strike came
when you told him you had enough.
You ended up in the hospital
because he was trying to be tough.
You hid the lies and abuse
from your family and friends.
Who knew so soon your life
would come to an end?
All the little marks that we never saw before
were covered by an excuse
like "you ran into the door."
Never knew he was knocking
you down to the floor.
I never understood why
abusers do the things they do.
But after a while you get tired
of being black-and-blue.
Right now, we are sitting here
reminiscing about you.
He abused you so much
because he thought you were creeping.
It broke my heart when your daughter asked,
"Is my mommy still sleeping?

So, you are gone now because you thought you were so much in love and all these memories are left behind.

So many men and women are in abusive

relationships and no one wants to talk, then when you see it on the news, you say to yourself, "you should have said something." Don't wait; if you see or know someone is being abused, call for help or try to get them help. Maybe you could have prevented it.

SO, FOR ALL YOU BATTERED WOMEN, REMEMBER YOU ARE NOT ALONE. LEAVE THIS RELATIONSHIP, GET HELP, PICK UP THE PHONE.

Don't let your parents plan a funeral too soon.

> *DEAR GOD... IT'S ME AGAIN, we need to talk. I can't sleep, because I just got the news that my friend/family member was killed. Why? What did she do? She was just here with me; we were at the laundromat and I said, "See you later." I did not mean in a coffin. Now the news is telling me she is dead! That is not how it is supposed to be. I hear and read about everybody else, but it never hit this close to home. Are you trying to tell me something? I don't know if I am coming or going. I know you are going to tell me she is in a better place. I know that. But when you get a chance, just watch over her for me, please, and tell her everything will be fine. I am tired of crying.*

STOP

IN MEMORY OF ....

*(A Mother, Sister, Aunt, Daughter,
Niece and Friend who had a bad fall)*

**For those who did not know her,
I have something to say
What I knew of her 'till this very day:
She was a friendly, funny,
athletic young mother
Who always made you laugh
and brought joy to others.
God was blessed with an angel
when he chose you,
But you were gone too soon –
what am I supposed to do?
I asked God to watch over you.
He said, "No problem!"
Because you know any problem we have,
only He can solve them.
I can't laugh, I can't smile;
dang girl, all I do is cry.
So many questions without answers
and I still ask why.
I wish that I could hold you;
I wish that I could touch you.
But you only left me memories
and a picture for me to watch you.**

Who can forget you with that beautiful smile?
That would stay with me
for more than a while.
Your beautiful smile was so bright.
Your laughter filled our life.
You were so much fun to be around;
you know this is true.
But dang...
why did this have to happen to you?
You were too young to die;
you didn't have to go.
We are really going to miss you,
more than you'll ever know.
You were so bright like a ray of sunshine.
With you in our hearts
we can leave life's troubles behind.
It is sad to see you go like this,
so for you, this is my last kiss.
Right now, I know you are in a better place,
But it is just hard to go on
without seeing your face.
This is the day of your final rest.
I would do anything in the world
to see your face again.
From your whole family
and all your friends:
We are all so sorry that your life
had to come to a tragic end.
I am not blaming you.
I know this was not your fault,
but I hope these women will learn
that when they are in a troubled relationship,
anytime, it could be their turn.
This is what can happen

STOP

***when a relationship goes wrong.
Love you girl; I love you so much.
I am trying not to cry,
but never in my wildest dreams
had I thought so soon
I would be saying goodbye.***

COLLEEN WILLIAMS

DID YOU HEAR ABOUT?

Did you hear about the man
that chopped off his wife's hands?
Did you hear about the husband
who forced his wife to drink acid?
Did you hear about the woman's body
they found on the beach?
She was mutilated.
I know you hear about the man
that kept threatening his wife
and she kept praying for him
and saying he will change soon.
Soon didn't come fast enough;
he slit her throat.
What about the woman
that was tired of the abuse,
so she left her husband
and went to live with her parents?
He found her, shot her,
and killed her in front her two kids.
Did you hear or see the video
that was circling the web a year ago
about the man who was kicking his woman
and hitting her with a knife,
while she was screaming on the ground?
Everyone was standing there
with their cameras recording it,

STOP

*posting it on social media, saying,
"I know him and that's what she gets."
Not one person tried to stop him
or called the police.
First of all: No, that is not what she gets;
it does not matter what she did,
no man or woman deserves to be abused.
So, now all these innocent children
that are left behind
do not have a mother or a father.
Not only that, now they have to be raised
with memories of their mother
being murdered, but the father is in jail.
It's sickening for me to see a man
beating his woman's ass
and she stays with him.
I am sure someone told them if they leave,
God will punish them.
I am sure someone told them,
"Oh, girl, he will change, just wait.
Y'all just need counseling. Pray for him."
Or the favorite one is:
"What did you do now to make him snap?"
It seems like the victims
are always the problem, ha?
I am sure someone said to them:
"What about the kids? He loves his kids.
Don't take them away from him.
I think you should stay."*

LADIES, AGAIN, Don't let anyone keep you where they won't stay. If a man is putting his hands on you, if he is beating your ass, degrading you, hurting you, it's time for you to go.

You can't reply from a coffin.

When you are listening to everyone else (who is not living your life) you will never hear your own self.

DON'T STAY, YOU RUN AWAY

Don't let your kids see him hit you, it will cause a serious problem later on.

I know not everyone has the strength to leave an abusive relationship.

You need to have strength and belief in yourself that you can stand alone and against all odds, stop thinking less of yourself.

Not everyone has the strength to leave.

Women need to believe in themselves and know that they are complete and whole individuals before the relationship, and they will be the same after it.

I'd rather live to tell a story and save another life.

I understand the whole idea of trying to intervene; you can get hurt, but we have to come up with a better solution than just standing there or even making it get this far. Because it's only when we are viewing the body at the funeral home we wish we could have done something or said something. I say "we" because as an advocate for Domestic Violence I am mandated by law to report any kind of abuse, but I have intervened and stopped over 20 domestic violence situations and every single one of them went back to their abusers and I looked like a complete fool.

I take this subject to heart because I know there is a woman out there that wants to leave an abusive relationship and she doesn't know how. Maybe she is scared, so I'm telling you now that you need to get up and walk away, make sure you go to a safe place. I don't know what triggers these men to trip off. I wish it can be so simple to just walk away. There are so many women in this world, if one don't want you, someone else will.

Women, I strongly suggest you get to know these men's background before you enter a relationship with them. Ask questions, do your homework. You chose to give them a part of you. I've had my share of Domestic Violence. I learned not to go by what they say. I go by actions. The first sign of them raising their voice or any type of control, I'm leaving.

I love myself too much.

I know you know someone who is involved in an abusive relationship. I know she calls your phone every night crying to you; maybe she talks in codes because she needs help and can't get out. You can't give up on them because the moment you give up and something bad happens, you will say, "Damn, I wish I was there for her."

TOO BROKEN TO BE FIXED

Ladies, don't ever think you are too broken to be fixed, because you are not. I need you to know your worth. You need to know and believe that you deserve happiness, love, trust, respect and honesty. You deserve nothing but the best. Once you know in your heart that you deserve better, once you know your worth, you will be able to walk away. You see, it happens. Be strong, don't keep allowing it, get out.

I listen to the stories I read in the newspaper. I know some of the victims. I've been to their funerals. I was a victim myself.

Nothing hurts me more than when a man beats his woman, chokes her till she can't breathe, tries to kill her, punches her in the stomach, makes her feel less of a woman, then when the police comes, she wants to cry and defend him in court, or bail him out. I can't understand it. Some men change; some don't. My job is to teach you how to protect yourself, how to know the signs. The yelling, the cursing, the name calling, he says he won't do it again, then he did it again, you give him a chance, he did it again. You have to think about yourself.

A lot of women are afraid of being rejected again, or having another failed relationship, so they try to work it out. They blame themselves, thinking it will get better. Yes, it will – the moment you leave, it will get better.

Don't get loved to death......

Me: Hey girl. What's up? What you doing here?
Friend: I just came from visiting my aunt. She is sick in the hospital.
Me: Okay, why you have on shades?
Friend: Girl, I just got my eyes dilated this morning.
Me: I meant to ask you the other day. I heard some noise upstairs. What was all that noise about?
Friend: Girl, we just got some new furniture, we were putting it away, redecorating.
Friend: I'm tired of lying, girl. I wear these shades because he punched me in my face again. We weren't putting away no new furniture. He was beating my ass again. I didn't go to visit my Aunt. I was just discharged from the hospital after he threw me out the car and left me unconscious again.
Me: Girl, why you stay with him?
Friend: He's all I know and he loves me.

Me: Wait, did you just say love? Listen, sweetheart. Love does not come with any black eyes, hospital visits or broken bones. Stop making excuses for him. Do you see him changing? I have known you for seven years and I have been telling you the same thing over and over again. Sis, please don't get loved to death. I already know if you stay it will get worse. If you leave, he might try to find you and hurt you. I'm not sure what other signs you are waiting for to leave.

MEN ARE VICTIMS TOO

I can't tell you how many men I know, or who I came in contact within my lifetime that also have been victims of domestic violence. I tried to help but they are the bread winners, they are holding it down, but the woman or wives are treating them like they are nothing. I can only give you a glass of water and put the glass in front of you, if you want to drink it then do, if not, then don't ask me for another glass. I tried to help, but the outcome was a mess.

I got a private phone call today from a guy telling me he had the chance to read my book; however, he was not pleased with my one-sided approach. He said I did not focus on men and domestic violence (still not sure how he got my number, but at that time, it was not important). I had to take the call because I get a lot of private calls and emails from a lot of women saying I inspire them to leave the abusive relationship they were in. But this guy was verbally abusing me, telling me he did not like what I wrote. So obviously, the woman that bought my book is abusing him. I said, "Sir, I apologize for what you are going through. I wrote about my experience what I went through while I was in a Domestic Violence relationship. I am not an expert in this field." He also added that she takes his money; calls him every negative name in the book. And when she hit him, he braces himself and she accuses him of hitting her. When he calls the police, they think it is a joke to hear a man is actually the victim. He was asked to leave the house; yes, the same house where he pays all the bills. She holds the kids over his head and threatens if he doesn't do what she wants, and then he can't see the kids. I talked to him; I gave him as much advice as I could but... in the end, I told him that there has to be someone out there that wrote a book about men being abused.

Trust me; I do understand that men get abused as well. I wish I can snap my fingers and make it stop for men and women. With all that being said, treat people the way you want them to treat you. Please know that men are also victims of domestic violence.

MY LITTLE SECRET

Mommy would always pick me up from school and drive around for a few hours before we go home. I like spending time with my mom. Although she listens to the weirdest radio stations, but hey, as long as she is happy, so am I. She is scared to go home because we both know what will happen. Robert (my dad) will hit her again. My dad is a drunk and every time he drinks, which is every day, he calls my mom all these bad names and starts slapping her around; when she tries to fight back, he hits her harder. I am always being told to go to my room. I think I read all the books in my room, then I look out the window wondering when it will stop. Is today the day that he kills her? When I hear my mom scream, I put my head under the pillow so I don't hear her because I feel bad because I can't help her. I block my ears so I won't hear her beg for help or beg for him to stop.

I even put the radio on loud so I can drown out her screams. I thought about peeking out my room door to run down the stairs and dash across the street to ask the neighbors for help, but I know he will catch me, drag me in my room, and take out his popsicle and make me suck it. Ooh, I wasn't supposed to say that. Yeah, he abuse me too. He abuse my mom physically and abuse me sexually. Mom don't know yet. I didn't tell her yet. Every time I try to talk, she always have something to do or somewhere to go. Then again, look what she has to deal with on an everyday basis; she have to worry about her safety.

I think my daddy don't like me or my mom; really he don't even like himself. He's always saying he is going to kill himself, but he never did. I really wish he would hurry up. I'm sorry, but I do. We don't have a good relationship. He chooses the bottle over his family. I don't remember any good times we had as a family.

Sometimes I sit on the stairs and look through the wooden bars while they are fighting. I shake my head and go back in my room. I said one day I have to tell someone this story. No one believes little kids. They think we are always lying or making up stories, but then when the truth come out, they say, "Oh, I'm sorry I didn't believe you before." Yeah, yeah, whatever.

It's been a long night of waiting, wondering and worrying. My mom (Katie) keeps peeping through the blinds to see when Robert (my dad) is coming home.

"Mommy, is Daddy coming home tonight?" I yelled.

"Why do you keep asking me that?"

"Because I want to tell you something."

"Well, young lady, I don't know if he's coming and I really don't care, but by you asking me the same question every hour on the hour will not bring him home any faster."

"If you don't know or care if he's coming, why do you keep looking out the blinds?"

"Kylee, please go get washed up for dinner," she said in a draining, aggravating, tiring voice. "Let me try calling again," she said as she picked up her phone, pretending to call. She never did make the call; she didn't want to be bothered with his drunk ass, the cussing, the arguing, and the abuse.

Thirty minutes later, I ran down the stairs and joined my mom at the table. "Yes, I love shrimp scampi," I said as I started to twirl the spaghetti on my fork. "Okay, Mommy, let's pray." We held hands. "Dear God, thank you for the world so sweet, thank you for the food we eat, thank you for the birds that sings, thank you God for everything. God bless the homeless people who don't have any food and bless my Mommy, and God, wherever my dad is, please let him stay there?"

"Kylee, that is not a nice thing to say."

"Well, you told me I can pray to God about anything, and all I have to do is trust in him and have faith that he will answer my prayers. So anyway, Mom, did you call him?"

"Yes, I did, but no answer."

"Mommy, you don't have to lie to me. I was at the top of the stairs. I know you are scared of him and you don't want him here. I don't want him here either."

"Kylee, why would you say such a thing like that?"

"Well, when he is here, he spends all his time beating you or finding something to argue about. Mommy, you can't make bad things go away by pretending they don't exist. I'm not stupid. I'm eleven. I'm growing up. I see it all."

My mom was a bit surprised to hear that coming from my mouth. I wasn't. "I'm actually tired of it. You can't keep hiding it and making excuses for him, Mommy."

I didn't even get to eat the food. I just lost my appetite. I pushed away my plate and left the table and stormed up the stairs. My mom followed behind.

"Kylee, please come back here. I can't

deal with this attitude you keep giving me."

"Listen, Mom." I stopped in the middle of the stairs and looked down at her. "If you want things to go back the way it was with us, then get rid of your husband." I continued up the stairs and went straight in my room.

My mom went in her room and cried. I woke up two hours later, disturbed by the excessive noise in my Mom's room wondering, what now? I got up to go see what was happening. To my surprise, I peeped through the already ajar door to hear mom saying: "Eneee meenie miney mo, should he stay or should he go?" while packing all his things in big jumbo garbage bags.

"If you have to ask that again, Mommy, then he should go," I said as I pushed the door open all the way. Mommy can see me through the mirror. She turned around and walked to me and held my hands.

"You know what, Kylee? You are so right. I can't keep living this life, trying to be a mother, a wife, and everything else. He is your father but once I see how this relationship is affecting you, then he has to go. If not for me, but for you, because I love you." We hugged each other tight for one minute, only tears, no words. I still had to find the time to tell her what he did to me.

I let go of my mom as we both heard the downstairs door rattling. It's him. Butterflies took their place in my stomach. I went back in my room to prepare myself for more yelling, more arguing, and putting my head under my pillow.

I don't even know what happened, but I know I woke up Monday morning and he was still there. Let's hope he was too drunk to even argue. I was dragging and hoping I would be late, because I'm really starting to hate school more and more every day. It's not school, it's just I find it extremely hard to concentrate when there's so much going on at home.

Well, I made it to school. Mommy dropped me off as usual. When I open my door, I always take a look at her to get an image of what she was last wearing just in case the police find her body somewhere.

"Love you, Mom."

"Love you too, Kylee."

After homeroom, my first class was art. The teacher, Mr. Massey, gave us 15 minutes free draw to draw what's on our mind. So, I drew my bed, my pillow, and my dad's popsicle in my mouth. I was done, so I put my head down on the desk. Mr. Massey was walking around the room, checking on our papers; he stopped at my desk and said, "What's this,

Kylee?" I told him when I'm in my room my dad gives me his popsicle to make me feel better. He said great job! He showed the class the picture. "Hey, class, look. Kylee's dad is great. He shares his popsicle with her." I got an A in his class. I think A stands for ass if he didn't understand what I was saying. That just went right over his head. I'm eleven. I know it was not a popsicle, but I wasn't going to go into details.

I went home and pretended I was sick so I wouldn't have to deal with my mom or dad. I tried to sleep till the next morning. That didn't work. My mom came in my room and woke me up. "Hey, baby girl, are you okay?"

"I'm fine, just drained."

"Okay, do you have any homework?"

"I did it in class."

"Kylee, that's why it's called homework."

"Well, I did it in class because if I come home, I know it won't get done here. You can't help me because you have a drunk... I mean, your husband to deal with, so I'd rather do it in class and get it over with."

She shook her head and walked out of my room. I am pretty sure I hit a nerve.

Tuesday morning... Of course, my dad was at the liquor store before it was open. My mommy made my lunch and took me to school.

I dreaded my first class which was gymnastics. I don't like this class. The teacher looks like my dad and he always has something stupid to say. He always runs his finger through my hair. He says it's soothing. I feel tingly and I wish he would stop touching me. Yuck! I'm only eleven years old. I want to play with my friends. I'm not trying to be an adult yet. If this is how men treat women or my dad treats my mom, I'd rather be single when I get older. I sat in a corner. I didn't want to be bothered. I always sit out in that class. I never participate.

Anyway, my favorite day is Wednesday – mother and daughter day. So, after school on Wednesdays, my mom always takes me to get ice cream. I love vanilla ice cream, especially with sprinkles.

I figured that would be the perfect time to tell Mom what Dad has been doing. I couldn't wait till 3:10, that's when the bell rings for the walkers; well I was a runner that day. As soon as I saw my mom's brown station wagon out front, I dashed out the door and jumped in the front seat. My mom always tries to beat the rush hour traffic to get to Friendly's. We got there and ordered my favorite, two scoops of vanilla ice cream on a cone with sprinkles. My mom got a bottle of water. I could tell something was on her mind, but I made up my mind she was going to listen to me today.

Mom asked, "How was your day today?" as we sat down on the patio chairs they had outside.

"Boring as always, Mom. I don't like school. I can't concentrate when I'm in school. I always wonder what are you doing? I can't wait till 3:10 so you can come pick me up. When I see your face, I always say "yes she's alive." That's how I feel. I never know when Dad will hit you so hard and knock you out and kill you." I continued eating my ice cream.

"Kylee, stop talking like that. I'm sorry. That should not be on your mind."

"Well, it is. You are my mommy and I love you. You are all I have. If or when Dad does something to you, then what?"

"I know, but what your dad and I go through has nothing to do with you."

"Really, Mommy? He hits you in front of me. I see it and hear it. I can't even help you because he will throw me out the way, send me to my bed, and then when he leaves you crying on the floor, he comes and puts his popsicle in my mouth." Oh boy, I said it. Yup, the ice cream just hit the fan.

"What did you just say, Kylee?" She spit out the water she just drank. A few observers looked in our direction.

"I said Daddy puts his popsicle in my mouth. I'm not supposed to tell you, but I'm getting sick of it. Mom, why are you crying?" I asked.

"I knew it," she screamed. "It's my fault!"

"It's not your fault, Mom. Dad is sick and he needs help."

"Kylee, come on, let's go," she said as she grabbed my hand.

"Wait, I didn't finish my ice cream!" She grabbed my hand so quick my ice cream fell on the floor. "Wait, Mom. Am I in trouble? Please don't tell Dad. He said it's our secret."

"Well, I got a secret for his ass, alright." My mom drove erratically from Friendly's straight to our house. I think she ran all the red lights. She jumped out of the car. She forgot I was still in the car.

She could see Robert's shadow through the kitchen curtain. She bust opened the door. "Let me tell you something, Robert." He tried to catch his fall from, of course, being drunk. "I let you abuse me, but when it comes to my child, you don't touch my child, you nasty bastard."

I came in the door, hiding behind my mom. "Sorry, Dad. I know it was supposed to be our little secret, but I had to tell Mom."

My Dad reached to grab me. "Kylee, come

here, you liar."

I never knew how brave my mom was until she placed her body between my dad and me. "Go in your room and lock the door. Do not come outside until I come and get you," my mom screamed, as I ran up the stairs. Mom waited to make sure my door was closed before she started to scold him. "Let me tell you something." She walked closer to him. (I was peeping out my door.) "I took your abuse, I took your blows, I took your beatings. I stayed for our daughter and you have the nerve to put your nasty little penis in her mouth. Drunk or not, you know better. She is your daughter, for God's sake. You need help. I'm leaving and taking my daughter."

"I did not touch her. She's lying. Who will you believe, her or me?" He slurred while stumbling, trying to catch his fall.

"Just get out now. I don't care where you go, just leave." I thank God he did not have a car, or it would have been a different story. Well, my dad left, no idea where he went; my guess would be the liquor store or his drunken friends' house.

I think yesterday was an eventful day, so my mom and I stayed home today, packing up my dad's stuff, while she was crying. I should have gone to school so she could get herself together, but then again I wasn't sure what he would have done to her. We waited for the locksmith to come and change the locks. After he gave us the new keys, I felt the weight lifted off my shoulders. I felt safe now.

Although I stayed home yesterday, I really did not want to go to school today (Friday), because every time you miss a day, everybody wants to know why you didn't come to school. Oh well, last day of the week is fun Friday. No homework!

In class, the teacher asked, "Are you all ready for Friday's reflection? Come on, on the rug. Let's go." The class headed to the rug with their notebooks to share their one reflection of the week.

"Who wants to go first?"

"Me, me, me!" Everyone had a story to tell. "I had a very interesting week..."

I didn't feel like sharing.

"Maritza, let's hear your reflection for today." Maritza stood up in front the class. "My grandparents came from Puerto Rico and they brought me a lot of things. They can't speak English very well, but my mom is happier because now she can get things done and have someone to help her out around the house to make things easier. I have fun teaching them English." Everyone clapped for Maritza.

"Well, alright Maritza. Great job, have a seat."

"Who's next? Conner, let's hear your reflection."

Conner stood up. "After my doctor's appointment Monday, my mom and dad took me to Olive Garden, so they didn't have to cook. When they get home sometimes it's hard when my mom and dad work late hours and then have to come home and cook and help me with homework. So, it worked out good for all of us. My favorite side order is the breadsticks and I get to dip it in the buttery garlic sauce."

"Okay, Conner, great job."

"Who's next?"

"Me, me, me!" Everyone's hands went up except mine.

Ms. Floyd looked over and saw me crying in the corner. "Kylee, are you okay? What's wrong, why are you crying?"

I blurted out, "Everyone has a good story to tell. I'm the only one who gets abused at home. When I went to get ice cream with my mom two days ago, I told her what my dad did to me. She got mad, went home and yelled at my dad. They argued. I went to my room as usual and I came to school. I don't want to go back home."

The whole class got quiet. It was either

too much for Ms. Floyd to take in, or they had no idea what the right answer would be. Ms. Floyd asked the Para to keep an eye on the class.

"Kylee, let's take a walk." She took me by my hand and we walked to the principal's office. Knock, knock, knock. "Hello, can I come in?"

"Hi, Ms. Floyd."

"Hi, we need to have a talk right away. Kylee, you know the principal, right?"

"Yes," I said between crying and wiping my eyes.

"Can you please repeat what you said in the classroom?"

"Will I get in trouble?" I asked.

"It's not about getting in trouble, our concern here is making sure you are safe. We just need to help you, that's all."

I tried to use some different words, but it doesn't matter how I tried to fix it, it's still wrong. "I want to go home, but I don't want my father there. He beats my mom every day and then he comes upstairs and tells me he wants to make me feel better and puts his penis in my mouth."

"Kylee, that's enough. Ms. Floyd, please, let's get her mother on the phone. I'll phone the department of social services and the police; we need to remove this child ASAP."

Everything was happening so fast, I had to sit down. I thought the room was spinning. Miss Anderson jotted down some notes on the desk calendar. Thank you, Ms. Floyd, you can return to your class. I looked around the office. I had an idea what was going to happen, but I didn't know it was going to happen so fast. I wanted to tell someone but didn't want my mommy to get in trouble.
"Hello, Ms. Schneider, this is the principal at the Beacon elementary school. I have your daughter in my office. She mentioned something in class that landed her in my office. Stories like this, we must take seriously; if we ignore it and something happens, then we will be held responsible. At this time, we will need to get CPS and a social worker and retain custody of Kylee until further notice."

I heard my mother's scream all the way through the phone. "Oh no, please, please, don't take my daughter." My mom got to my school so fast, either she was on her way here, or there were no cars on the street. She was still on the phone when she came to my school. She could see police and Department of Children Protective Services car already outside. She had no idea her biggest fear was about to happen.

While my mom was entering the building, CPS was escorting me out of the school entrance. My mom could only watch as I was being ripped away from her.

She tried to reach out and hug me. "I'm sorry, Kylee," she cried softly. "I'm so sorry." They just kept walking me to the car. The kids in my class and other students were looking out the window. What a bad memory they will have of me.

"Ms. Schneider, please come inside." That was the last thing I heard.

But when I got to my new spot, they told me my mom had to get rid of my dad or move out and find a suitable and safe place for me to stay. They gave her 30 days to get the rest of her stuff together, like take parenting classes and counseling. In the meantime, we would be able to see each other once a week. The sad thing about abuse is the abuser never has to go through any of these things, always the innocent victims.

I really don't want my stay here to be long. I spent the weekend in my room and went to school every day as usual. Apparently, we are not allowed phone calls, but we are allowed to get letters. I slept the whole weekend away. I came out a few times to eat and went right back in my room. It's been one full week here.

STOP

The following Monday afternoon I got my first mail. I knew it was my mom. I guess she wrote it Friday and mailed it Friday, because it got here quick.

> Hello, Kylee.
>
> I came in Friday night and went to sleep. I woke up thinking it was a dream that you got taken away from me. I yelled out your name, but you never answered. I thought you were still asleep. So, I walked in your room and the bed was made up just how you left it. I totally forgot you were gone. It's still a nightmare but I won't waste no time. I'm going to do what I was ordered to do to get you back to me asap. I wonder what you are doing. Are they treating you good?
>
> Did you sleep last night? I stayed awake wondering if you were okay.
>
> I'm not worried. I'm more shocked that I allowed this to happen. I promise we'll be together very soon. I will do everything in my power, even if I have to walk to the moon. Kylee, I miss you every single day and I never had a good night's rest since they took you away.
>
> I will come see you on our favorite day, Wednesday. I'm doing all the necessary steps to get you back with me asap. You don't have

to write back; we can talk when I see you.

Love, Mom.

The day has finally come when I get to see my mommy. Every day a new child was coming in. So sad to see how children are being taken from their parents. My mom took that long, one-hour drive to come see me.

They called my name, Kylee Schneider. I felt so important. I walked out the room and straight to the big open space I looked around and saw other parents visiting their children. My mom snuck up behind me. I jumped and held her tight.

"Oh my gosh, I missed you so much." She started crying.

"Mommy, please no tears. So, tell me, what have you been doing? First of all, is Dad finally gone?"

My mom took out a check list. I thought she was about to write a grocery list, but it was a list of things she had to do in order to get me back.

- Get rid of dad. (She already did that.)
- Take parenting/counseling class.
- Take self-defense class.
- Show proof that she is active in my life. (She does all the bake sale and parent council

meetings at my school.)
- Last, but not least, prove that it is safe for me to come back home. (My mom changed the locks and kicked him out and removed all his belongings. I know, we did it together.)

"Wow, Mom. I am so proud of you, you move very fast."

"Well, Kylee, it's called a mother's love. I would fight for you any day, but if you had told me sooner, you would not be here. I would have taken care of it right away."

"What do you have there?" my mom asked.

I smiled and handed her a letter. She handed it back and told me to read it to her. All you can see was smiles on both of our faces. I sat down across from my mom. "Okay, let's go."

Hi, Mom!

It was strange getting a letter from you when you usually come in my room to talk, but anyway, although you told me don't write back, I wanted to. I'm okay. I miss you. It's weird going to school, being dropped off and picked up by strangers, when I'm used to you doing it. But it's a lot of us here, so I can imagine what other people go through. I did not make any friends. I don't want to meet anyone. In order for me to come back home I think you should get rid of daddy once and for all. Stop feeling sorry for him and letting him back in. He does not know how to be a dad or a husband. I know you are worried about me but if dad is gone it won't make a difference. He serves no purpose when he is there anyways. If you stay and he kills you, then I won't have a mother or a father.

At school I see a lot of my friends' mothers and fathers come to pick them up but that don't mean they are happy. It can be a cover up. I want to come back home but not with dad there. My grades are dropping. I don't sleep at night. I sleep all day in school. This is getting really tiring, so mommy please, if you want a better relationship with me, can you please leave daddy? If he don't want to get help, then you get help. Anyway, I have to go now. I'll see you soon.

Love you.

"That was so sweet. I am just admiring my little girl growing up so quickly."

"Well, Mommy, we don't want history to repeat itself. I would love to get married one day. I know I'm only eleven, but in eleven years when I'm an adult and I start dating, how would you feel if I call you and tell you my boyfriend keeps beating me? You wouldn't like it, so if this is all I am seeing from you and my dad, then you can't get mad when another man does the same thing to me so now is the perfect time to stop the cycle."

"Listen, Kylee, I understand you. I'm not sure how many times I can apologize to you, but I came here to tell you I did everything on the list. I took all my classes and your dad is no longer there. I don't know where he is. Right now, I'm just waiting for social services to say I'm all set to take you home. Some people take months to complete it; I took a week and a half."

I notice a lot of officials in the room. I guess they are monitoring the visits. I looked over my mom's shoulder and one of the ladies who was at my school came and put her hand on my mom's shoulder and said, "You can take your daughter home now. I never saw a mother do everything on that list the way you did. We gave you 30 days. You did it all back to back in less than two weeks. Ms. Schneider, please stand up." She gave my mom a certificate of completion.

"For real? For real?" I jumped up. I didn't want to get too excited, because a lot of the kids were not getting to go home with their parents. I was excited but had to respect them. My mom knees were shaking. I think all the tears she held back from the abuse, all the times she wanted to cry and couldn't, even when they took me away. She had sleepless nights. I think now she was able to cry and let it all out.

I went in my room and packed up the little bit of things I had. OMG, I can actually sleep in my own bed tonight. We thanked everyone that helped us. I slept so good, I woke up late the next morning. My mom transferred me to a new school because it would have been a lot to deal with. Children see a lot of things and don't understand so they make up stories, but I knew if I went back to that school, it would have been very traumatic for me. I'm ready for a brand-new start. My mom and I are in counseling for what my dad put us through. My mom has a full-time job, so she's not at home waiting in fear. And to be honest, I have no idea what happened to my dad.

SEXUAL ABUSE

I was left in Trinidad for four years from age 9 to 12, and four years straight, this man sexually molested me. I had nowhere to turn. I had no family.

BEING SEXUALLY ABUSED

*(The memories are shaky,
but it's coming back to me.)*

*I wrote many poems in life,
but this one was the hardest to write.
Because after so many years,
I still stay up at night.
To memories of being
sexually abused as a little kid.
I wish these people would go to hell
for what they did!
Being sexually abused is not a good feeling.
Your mind and body needs a lot of healing.
I've been there before and believe me, it hurts.
How does it feel to have a man
put his hand up your skirt?
How does it feel when something wouldn't fit?
Let me be the one to tell you!
It feels like ish!
How does it feel
when you don't want to be touched?
I hate that feeling so darn much.
Memories of me being in that situation
for four painful years.
These people destroyed my life;*

STOP

left me drowning in tears.
Every day I left the house, I asked God,
"Is this the end?"
But when I came home from school,
the abuse was on again.
I remembered, I came home from school
and said I was sick.
You put me in a room
and made me play with your manhood.
I can't forget that I was nine
and you were forty-three.
All that was on your mind was to screw me.
In the doctor's office even,
the doctor started to cry.
She asked, "Has anyone touched you?"
You know I had to lie.
Well the abuse stopped around 1983.
That's because I'd had enough, you see.
There is nothing I can do now; it's too late.
But the one word I can use is HATE!
This unwanted, sexual, forceful, penetration
Led me to a lifetime of frustration
Dealing with so much aggravation,
I just wanted to hide from the whole nation.
Bear with each other
and forgive whatever grievance
you may have against one another.
Forgive as the Lord forgave you.
                                                           Col. 3: 13

BEHIND THE WINDOWS OF MY SOUL

    I never thought my first time would hurt so much. It's all because of you I don't wear shorts. It's all because of you I don't expose my body. It's all because of you I had bad relationships. I hated men for so long because I thought they were all like you. I am still bitter; I blame all men for your mistakes. You messed up my life in every way possible. You took something that was very precious to me. {My childhood} I know in order to be right with God I have to forgive and forget so..... I forgave you, but will not forget it. A lot of people keep telling me I am grown; I need to get over it. You get over a crush, a broken heart, but someone messing with your life daily; that is not something you forget. You will remember that for the rest of your life. It hurts, it really does.
    I remember lying in the bed at night and when I heard your footsteps coming down the hallway, I would close my eyes and cover my head with the sheets to pretend I was sleeping so you would turn around and leave me alone,

but you didn't. I remember family would call to talk to me and you would never let me speak to them; you would always find excuses not to put me on the phone so they would not find out the shit you were doing. I have nothing but bad memories. I remember when I went to the store and took too long – you would meet me halfway and beat me all the way home. Right now, I have a big burn on my left hand where you threw scalding water on me because I stole a cookie. I stole it because you refused to feed me. If anyone sees it, I tell them it is my birthmark because I am too ashamed to tell them what really happened. I was at a workshop and their icebreaker was, "Who Stole the Cookie from the Cookie Jar?" As soon as they started, tears formed in my eyes. I had a nervous breakdown and an anxiety attack because it reminded me of the time, I stole the cookie. I can't even stand in front of a mirror and smile; I look like I just walked through a battlefield. I am lucky to be alive. Give me one good reason why you did what you did.

    You see, you only left scars and pain that I have to deal with every day of my life. All I ever wanted was an apology or an explanation. I know I will never get it; so what am I waiting for? It's messed up – the abuse and neglect I got when I was in your care. I have to sit here and try to figure out all the answers to the questions I have. Why should I blame myself? I didn't do anything. I always thought it was something I did; but no, I was being a little innocent child. I didn't ask for this. All I wanted was love and guidance. What can I say now, at this age? I can only pray that you don't do it to anyone else. Things like this stay with you forever. What if someone did that to your mother, your sister, or your daughter? How would you feel? Would you want to find them and rip their insides out? Would you want them dead? I know how you would feel because I want to do the same thing to you. You made sure when I left the house, I was nice and clean to go to school – something like a cover up! I tried to tell someone, but I couldn't. But like they always say, "No one knows what happens behind closed doors."

Why do I need to feel bad about myself? I didn't abuse me; you did. Yes, it has been over 30 years; what makes you think I would stop the tears? I have a son now and sometimes when I have tears in my eyes, he asks me, "Mommy, why are you crying?" What am I supposed to say to him? He wouldn't even begin to understand. I look at him every day and I pray to God that no one touches him. I do not want him or no one to go through what I had to go through. It's not a nice feeling – trust me, I know. I kept it a secret. I played it off so no one would know the scars all over my body that I am scared to show. I was an actress for years. My eyes flooded with tears; dealt with this secret for so many years. No one saw my fears. I said to myself, "no one cares." No one deserves to be touched (abused) or raped. Now I am left to put these pieces back together by myself. So, you see, at the tender age of nine, I was left to ask questions that no one was able to answer and now, I am okay enough to write about it. I was too young at the time to talk, but I can talk now; I have questions now. You want to know if I will forgive you - yes. God forgave me, so I forgave you.

God chose (hurt, loneliness, heartache, mistakes,) the weak things of the world to shame the strong.
1 Cor. 1:27

HE SAID SHE SAID

He said if I tell anyone he will kill me.
I didn't want to die so I didn't tell.
I hid that secret very well.
He asked me how I feel. I said fine.
What the hell do I know? I was nine.
I said I will tell my mother,
he said he didn't care,
if she cared about you
she would have never left you here.
Now allow me for one moment
to get things clear,
and I don't give a damn
who I anger in here.
But how can a mother sleep good at night
knowing something with her daughter
just isn't right?
He thought this was a joke
but I had to keep playing,
didn't know my innocence
was actually straying.
They say stop talking about it, let it go,
sweep it under the rug.
They didn't know all I wanted
was a simple hug.
They lie when they said one size fits all.
These nasty perverts

STOP

touching children from small.
Years built up of anger,
this thought never left my mind.
I wish someone can take away all my pain,
so I would never have to go through stress
again, no more walking in the rain.
Time to break these chains.
Wish there was less to lose
and more to gain.
No more waiting in vain,
wishing things can go back to normal
or being the same.
I just need you to know
you don't have to be ashamed.
Sexual abuse is not a game.

MY LIFE MATTERS, SO I SPOKE UP

*I tried to tell someone,
but nobody wanted to help.
I went in a room
and started writing to myself.
All I wanted to say was I was date raped.
He put me in a room
and covered my mouth with tape.
It started out with a date, a laugh,
jokes, and then a tickle.
Then he decided to pull out his pickle.
He then proceeded
to put his pickle in my mouth.
That didn't work so he went down south.
Right there, I knew something wasn't right.
I pushed him off me with all my might.
He stumbled backwards,
tripped, and hit his head.
That was my chance to jump out the bed.
I ran out the room, straight out the door.
But he got hold of me
and threw me on the floor.
He felt because he was bigger than me
he was going to win
But this little warrior
had a lot of fight within.
He called me everything in the book*

STOP

except my name.
Then he said I was to blame.
He said my shirt was too tight,
my skirt was too short,
and I looked like a tease.
I said to myself, "boy please."
A friend told me I put that on for show.
She is missing the point: no means no.
I wish you would stop telling me
to get over it, it didn't happen to you.
If you were in my shoes,
you wouldn't know what to do.
It doesn't matter what you wear
or how you look.
If you don't want to give it up, then don't.
When you say no is no,
don't give in to make him win.
Don't say yes to make him happy.
Because when you leave you will feel crappy.

HE TOUCHED ME

I have been trying to tell my mother this for over 20 years.

I came to you; I told you what happened when you left me in Trinidad. You ignored me year after year. I found many ways to tell you. Mom, remember the guy you left me with in Trinidad? He touched me. Someone close to you told you what happened to your daughter; you ignored it. Many people told me I need to talk to a specialist. Sorry, but 45 minutes every two weeks can't fix this lifetime pain. When I slept with a man, I felt like I was being raped all over again. I came back and said, "Okay, this is it – maybe you will hear me this time." But again, you were in denial. Conversations changed. He came to me at the tender age of nine. He was older than me; he knew what he was doing. Maybe this is what he has been doing for a while, so he came to me as an innocent child. I was a victim of sexual abuse. Why should I sit in silence? I need to let my voice be heard. If I don't speak up, nothing will change.

I held in every bit of strength inside of me, not to reach over and grab your ass so I can shake some sense in you.

LISTEN WOMAN, he touched me. I was taking a bath outside and he came, stood there, and looked at me. I grabbed whatever I could have grabbed to cover myself, but he just stood there. I thought it was a mistake, but he heard the water running, so he knew I was there. He showed no remorse; he didn't care. It seems like no matter what I say, no matter what stories I write, you don't care, huh? I made a decision when I got older, I will take it upon myself to go look for him and ask him why? I did get older; I did go look for him, but when I got to the area, I just stood at the bottom of the hill with my hands on my hips and looked up. (Boy, do I remember that hill.) That was the same hill I walked to and from school; walking up that hill to his house was like signing my own self up for execution. People still remembered me as the little skinny, nappy-head girl who was being sexually abused; to make a long story short... he was already dead.

Yeah, that's what I said. I doubled over, hands on my stomach just crying; not sure what I was crying for. I was happy and sad at the same time; happy he won't be able to hurt another innocent child and sad because I still never got any answers from him, because talking to you is like watching paint dry... very boring, no life, just there. But at the end of the day, just know that he... touched... me.

A LETTER TO THE MAN WHO MOLESTED ME

It took me years to write this letter to you. I know you are no longer on this earth, but I need this pain to go away once and for all. I didn't have the words before, or the clarity, or the courage. But today I do. Today, I can see how my life has changed from then to now.

I don't want to go into details about what you did; you knew what you were doing. I just wanted to know why? All I remembered was every night before bed you always put me to sit on your lap and telling me to open my legs, so you can pull my underwear aside and stick your finger inside of me, then you said give you a kiss; when I reached in to give you a kiss on your cheek, you turned your face so it can land on your mouth, so disgusting. I really hated sitting on your lap because I knew what was going to happen. Then you said go to my room. I thought I did something wrong, not knowing you were about to finish what you started. You would creep into my room and force your manhood inside of me and satisfy yourself. I felt so nasty when I got up and had to go outside. I thought everyone can see what you did. I didn't understand it, I was confused.

That was not the only time you touched me. It happened many times after that, but you know that already. I remembered you told me don't let anyone see my little box but you. I went to school and told my friends, "Hey my uncle told me you can't touch my little box." They were laughing because no one knew what the hell I was talking about. I even asked my friend, "Hey, does your uncle touch your little box, like my uncle touched mine?" She said what? I pointed down to my little box. She looked lost and confused.

My mom had called and I told her you touched my little box. She changed the subject right away saying she loved me and missed me. I said if you love me, come get me, where are you? She said she will come get me soon. I was wondering did she hear me, or did she ignore me like the last time I told her that her other boyfriend touched my box.

I told the teacher about my little box and she told the nurse. The nurse said I'm a liar, I made it up; I was just looking for attention.

After school, here we go again, back to your house and it continued. I wanted to tell you wife what happened, not knowing she was going to be a part of this later on that night. I had no way out, no escape, no one to tell. My mother is already gone; it was just me and my secrets. I couldn't run away. I was too little. I did leave after four terrible years and that never left my mind.

Now I hear it is happening all over the world. I wish I could kick down the door and save these innocent children. So, you are not the only sick, nasty bastard that goes around doing this to innocent children. I did forgive you for what you did, because I knew it was a sickness that made you do it. It has taken my whole life to finally forgive you and my mother. I spent years seeking help. I was so messed up mentally for so many years; I was on all different types of medication. So much has happened in the past 30 years. I still don't even know who to blame: my mom for leaving me there, or you for knowing what you were doing and not caring.

I kept it a secret, because it seems like the more people I told they all said I was crazy, which caused more pain, because to hold on to that for so long and never get an answer is devastating.

I spent my whole life feeling disconnected from the world. I couldn't trust anyone. I was always covered up. I would wear underwear, leggings, then my pants. I just wanted to protect myself so it wouldn't be so easy for another man to just open my legs and take what he wanted. I've battled with my relationships, my trust, my life, my son, my weight, because I wasn't able to see myself clearly. I spent my entire life feeling damaged because of a few years you took from me for your own satisfaction.

I am grateful I was able to get away to seek help to get over the sick feeling.

I know that everything happens for a reason. I wanted to bleach myself so I could wash away the nasty feeling I get when you cross my mind.

Because I lived with this pain for so many years, every time I see my mom I want to ask her why, but with her being in denial, I knew I was never going to get an answer, so it was back to square one with unanswered questions. Not sure why this was a secret. Why was I left to ask so many questions?

30 years now, I'm blessed. I'm strong, independent, resilient, and unstoppable because of what you did to me when I was a young. I really love the woman I am today, and I know that even the most unpleasant parts of my past have brought me to this moment. As I sit here and reflect on my past, I shake my head. I hate the fact that it happened. However, I'm grate-

ful to have this story to share, because I know there are so many more people just like me who are hurting and still struggling with the after-effects of childhood abuse. I'm glad I can help them.

I put my life on hold. I didn't want to continue until you told me why, but I have to remember it is done and I am not going to get an answer, so it's time to shift my focus on helping others instead of hurting. I blamed myself for so many years this, was a hard pill to swallow.

Yes, you took my childhood, my innocence, my virginity (I guess you can call it that). But, you never broke my spirit.

I have faced every challenge and overcome every obstacle. I am a stronger woman today for having been victorious in these battles.

I had to let go. I had to stop holding on. You are no longer here. I forgave you a long time ago, but I wanted to sit down face to face to tell you how I felt. I will never forget what you did to me. I will continue to share my story, in hopes that it will help someone else who shares my struggle.

At my age now, painful memories have been haunting me real bad. They said it's been so many years, but they don't understand. I wish someone had saved me or came to my rescue.

I just wanted to ask why? I was a child. What did I do? Why me? Are there any more people who are hurting like me? I can't explain it to anyone, they were not there.

People say, "Girl, stop holding on. Get over it." My face turns red every time someone tells me to get over it. {They can't tell me how I feel.} Their mother did not leave them with a stranger or uncle or whatever you were. I will be fine. I will stop asking why and what did I do? I tried to let it slip from my mind, vanish from my thoughts, but it keeps haunting me that you touched me. I saw an old man the other day just raking his yard, minding his own business, and I did a double take. He looked just like you, but I know it wasn't.

You made me do a pinky promise not to tell.

I spent my entire life walking this earth, thinking I was to blame, hiding my face, feeling ashamed. Despite it taking me days, weeks, months and years, I finally realized I'm not the same little girl that was scared in your house.

I didn't know what was going on, but I knew it wasn't right.

I thought you were a good person by taking me in, because my mother didn't want me or whatever reason I was there.

Now that you are dead, I have to put this pain to rest and the nightmares are gone.

Most recently, someone special came into my life. I told him what happened, but he only sees the brightness in me. He makes me realize it was not my fault. I need to let go of the past. He has taught me that holding on for so long is a waste of time because I can't do anything about it. He makes me laugh; he can see the beauty in me. I was in a very dark place. I wish he came into my life sooner; if he had said it sooner, I would have let go long ago. So glad I can finally let go, it's time to let go.

If my story can help anyone who has been sexually abused, anyone who has been left with unanswered questions, anyone can read my story and teach them how to heal from childhood sexual abuse, I'm happy to share it. If just one person can benefit from these words, I am grateful to have written them.

I was scared and alone as a little kid. Every night tears were falling down this nine-year-old face when you came in the room. I wiped it with my pillowcase.

When your wife was sleeping or left the house, all of a sudden you wanted to play cat and mouse. You would sneak in my room and get on your knees; you felt it was cute to touch my cheese.

You put me in your little perverted world just to mess up an innocent girl; you messed up my entire world.

It's sad you got away with what you did, touching and raping an innocent kid.
I wish I could find you and make you pay for what you did to me that day.

I was asking questions for many years since the pillowcase wiped my tears.

I won't get an answer because you are now dead, but this is something that will never leave my head.

~ Colleen Williams

STOP

TAKING BACK MY POWER

When you have been victimized, raped, taken advantage of, in a domestic violence relationship, you feel like you have no strength to fight.

But if you are here today, guess what? You had enough strength to get up, get out, and stand up for what you believe in. Today I am taking my power back and holding my head high.

*He took away my voice,
I was young I had no choice.
Although I said no, he took it as a yes.
Constant memories of his hands
sliding up my dress.
He left me as a victim
but now I am a survivor.
Yeah, he hurt me, he made me cry,
but today I'm holding my head up high.
Can't believe this man
had a hold over me for 20 years.
I kept my body covered,
I had so many fears.
I was told to get help,*

but one 45-minute session a week
can't begin to heal this lifetime pain.
I wanted to go in the corner
and never come out again.
I almost gave up,
but I remembered I had a story to tell.
I remember I'm here to inspire a victim
and make her a survivor, a warrior.
For the ones who can't speak up
because they don't get that choice,
I'm here to be that voice.
I couldn't give up
without you hearing my story.
This is why I say
to God be the glory.
I have to deal with a mother
who is still in denial
that someone touched her innocent child.
I constantly remind myself
it will be over soon;
today I'm a black beautiful butterfly
emerging from a cocoon.
My voice is my talent I will forever use.
Please speak up
if you have been sexually abused.
I am a woman, I'm proud, I'm strong.
I refuse to remain a victim.
I will not be silent anymore.
Today, I'm taking my power back
and holding my head up high.

I SURVIVED!!!

I was young and naïve, didn't know much, innocent young girl who was touched. I lost my innocence.

I blamed myself for everything that happened to me, but I was wrong. I was the victim; it was never my fault.

I was always brave and strong. But my abusers held me down.

I thought I would never find anyone to love me, to understand me, or to listen to me, understand where I came from, and what happened to me.

I know one day soon I will be strong again.

I know I will be brave again; I have to be.

I will be in love again. And he will love me back. He won't hurt me, he won't hit me, he won't abuse me.

I won't give up, I will make it through.

One day I will be smiling and celebrating and overcoming everything that happened in my life. I am strong. I always fight back and when I do, I won't fall down again. I am like a ball; I hit the bottom and always bounce back up. This time I'm staying up. I always win.

No matter what I have been through, I am here.

My inner strength, something about me shined bright. I was not going to allow anyone to destroy me anymore. I continued growing stronger within, and I will continue to keep evolving, learning, striving, to be the best me I know how.

I will continue to walk into my destiny with my head held high, because I know I have God walking by my side.

I will make this world a better place.

I have survived!!!

YOU ARE NOT ALONE, AND IT WASN'T YOUR FAULT

I want to end this on a positive note to all women, any race, any color, as long as you are a woman.

I am speaking and writing this from my heart. Yes, everything you read about me was true. I went through it all and worse. A lot more happened that I can't even write about, but I was involved in the worst four relationships in my entire life.

Please don't take risks. Don't think it won't happen. It's not pick and choose; when a man wants you dead, he will do what he has to do. Don't ever think he has his abuse under control. If you and he are getting help together and you can see improvements, then you make that call, but don't automatically play Miss Know-it-all and try to fix a man. I don't want you to think I'm coming down on all men, but I am only speaking about the men that abuse their women. Trust me, they have some good men out there. After four failed relationships, I thought to myself, "No man will want a broken woman, but I hope my future husband will understand that none of my abuse was my fault."

Please don't beat yourself up for not walking away sooner.

You were preyed upon. You are the victim, you were innocent, something is wrong with them. They knew you had nowhere to go; they made you promise you would not tell because they knew they were doing something wrong. Don't worry no more, don't cry, don't question it, you didn't do anything.

Seconds, minutes, hours days that turned into weeks, then months, and then years. Don't dwell on it, don't think, don't analyze, don't try to remember what happened, let it go. You are out. You got away, you made it, you survived it. I'm proud of you.

They chose to make your life a living hell. They tried to keep you away from the ones who loved you. They brainwashed you. They say they will protect you. How can they protect you when they are hurting you? They target the weak and innocent ones who can't protect themselves.

Let me tell you something about these abusers.

They don't want you to have any friends, any kind of contact, no one to talk to. No social media, no phone, because they know if they get caught then their game is over.

So now you had to suffer your whole life as a broken child, into a teenager, into an adult. It was hard to explain to people because not everyone understands childhood sexual abuse

You suffered deeply. You isolated yourself, you started speaking out slowly and eventually someone wanted to listen.

So, keep telling your story, keep reaching out, never give up, don't hold it in. You are not alone; there are others waiting to hear from you.

Don't hide behind the computer screen. Don't look at someone else, saying, "I can't do that." Yes, you can, you can do it and do it better.

Some people hold it in and take it to the grave with them. Let someone know you were touched... or raped. We need to know, the more we know, the more we can fight for it, if it reaches one household, then yes, we did it.

I need you to know how special you are and I believe in you as a person.

You were born with a gift of love and laughter. Let the world see your smile. Keep shining. Don't let the world change your perspective and see things through their eyes.

Please know life will be challenging, but

you can do it. Have patience and understanding. Shine bright. We know that obstacles will come in your way but you have to knock them down one by one.

Get up and say, "I can and I will" and you will be able to do anything you put your mind to doing. Watch who you have around you. There are a lot of users out here and they will use you as long as you let them.

You are determined and dedicated. I believe in you.

Things happen. Don't shut down but take it with a grain of salt and fight back. You can and will do it. You can achieve anything you want!

Know that you are here for a reason. God makes no mistakes.

I am very proud of you and believe in you. You came this far. You made it but this is not the end. The sky is the limit. Never stop reaching, never stop learning.

Please remember it's not your fault. I don't know you, but I love you!

A PRAYER

Dear Lord,

Thank you for always making a way when there seems to be no way. No matter what I went through, you were there. Thank you for reminding me when I'm at my lowest to look to my highest and that is you. Thank you for the many blessings you have bestowed upon me as I continue on this journey. I never thought I would see the day where my storms are no longer cloudy, never thought I would see the light at the end of the tunnel. I never understood the meaning of faith but when I began to pray, not just some time but all the time, I started feeling the layers of my pain peel off, I started seeing people leaving my life and making my vision clearer for me to see where you were taking me. Every time I reached a tough situation I said "what did I do now? Why did this happen to me?" But it had to happen in order for me to grow. This test you put me through was a reminder of me going to school; I had to study and learn in order to pass the test. But with you I passed the entire test packet you gave me with flying colors. You had faith in me; you knew I could have done it if I only believed in you.

ACKNOWLEDGMENTS

My son Colin Williams... Keep reaching for the stars and never give up no matter what, continue to make me proud.

Derrick Ochro Williams. Your continuous prayers through my pain and suffering kept me going. Every time I wanted to give up, you were not having it. I was at the end of the rope and was about to throw in the towel, you kept me lifted in prayer. I thank you for being there for me. May God continue to bless you the way you bless others.

Natasha Moore @Msmooreproductions. Thanks for being an amazing sister and friend, thank you for always being there for me when I needed you the most. Your inspirational posts and your messages keeps me uplifted. Love you always.

Miss Stacey Hazeth @sexieredzz, getting to know you was like looking in the mirror. We go through so much in life, but we hold it in. You are such a beautiful person inside and out; may you continue to be the best that you can be. I am praying all your dreams come through, remember anything you put your mind to do you can do it.

Eric Thompson, My husband and best friend. Who would ever have thought I would be here today writing about you? I will never forget the first day we talked, I was so negative, I was giving you a one-word answer. I pushed you away and you just stood there. I shut you out before you had a chance to say hello. The day we met I knew you were real. Although I was skeptical and of course had my doubts, I told you I'm not looking for anything because I'm tired of getting hurt, and you refused to give up. You came into my life at the right time; you only wanted what was best for me; you always pushed me to be the best I can be. You have been with me through this rough ride. Thanks for holding on with me. Thank you for turning my frown upside down. Thank you for proving to me you are nothing like the rest. I know I have a friend in you forever. I never had to question your motives. I remembered I was sitting in a corner after failing so many times, I gave up. I got knocked down. I was numb; you took me by the hand and said, "We will do this together." That powerful word WE simply took the cake. I love our conversation; it makes us stronger every day. I hope and pray that God continues to be a part of our lives. No words in the dictionary can explain you. Sometimes you leave me speechless by your actions. Thanks for being a part of this journey, thanks for holding my hand through it. Thank you for listening to me nag and annoy you day after day to get this book done. Thank you for believing in me and my message. You had long days at work, sleepless nights, band practice, but you listened to my stories. You have inspired me to be the woman I am and the woman I'm still becoming. The best is yet to come, right? Don't forget our little bet. Love you forever, my bff.

Seasoned woman /Danita Biggs. It started with a t-shirt and you never left my side, you kicked down my door, you dragged me out of depression, you made me believe in myself, you were not taking no for an excuse. I did not want to do anything, I did not care anymore, everyone already used me and abused me. I settled for that. I told you there was no way I would be able to get back up after this mess, but you were not having it. You told me I could do it. I said I will but I stayed in my bed. You forced me to get my ass up and shine. You remind me I am the bomb.com and I am blessed that God sent you to remind me who I was.

If you were ever there for me, negative or positive, I thank you.

To the fake friends who betrayed me, I

thank you for making me stronger...

To the people who said they had my back but all I saw was your back when you walked away, I thank you. I thank God you never made it into my future..

For everyone that walked away, no worries. God replaced you with real people. I was never accepted, I was always rejected, I never fit, but I forgot God made me to stand out.

To my bosses and supervisors at both jobs who were always there for me. Mark, Bill, Jason, Paul, Gregg, Marybeth and all my co-workers, too many to mention. I thank you for making me feel like I was someone. When I was being called the "N" word, y'all had my back when no one else was there, y'all were. When I wanted to quit because I couldn't take the name calling y'all had my back. When I was hungry y'all made sure I was all set. To Miss Casey at the Opera House, thank you for holding me back when I wanted to quit. I appreciate you.

Marybeth, Shannon, Sharon and Amanda, Margaret Butters, Donna Prisco.

Cedric Quarles (Orpheum theater)

Dathan Rice: When I was being called the "N" word you had my back; you taught me how to stand up for myself and remember who I am and where I came from.

Tyrell Todd, you reminded me I am more powerful than I really know.

To Tanieka Whyte for your love your support. You inspire me to be a better person and go after my goals.

To my friend Free Smith, you are always there when I need to talk. You have uplifted me and kept me going. I appreciate you.

To my boy Charlie Franklin, you are just a bag of fun; you keep me going.

Thanks for the laughter. Love you all tremendously. Always remember to keep striving to be the best you can be. Never give up.

Thank you to all my Instagram family who have been my biggest cheerleaders. You all have been my reason to keep going.

Thank you for always supporting me through everything that I do.

Please know without you there would be no me.

Susie from Sister With Purpose, Inc, Brooklyn N.Y. You have always supported me from day one.

Nordholm Khayam Clark from Columbus Ohio, you already know we are friends till the end.

Shyne Creations/DeAnte` Piper for getting me back in the swing of things.

Hillary Chamblee/No Regret Ministries

Due to my past with church folks I could not go back to church or trust anyone. I was having anxiety attacks when I passed the church, but you told me I'm going to church to hear the word of God not for other people. It's a work in progress but I'm getting there.

    Hope Renea B. Thank you for helping me with my weight loss journey and just being yourself.

    Darryl Bourn /Roanoke Rapids NC.

ABOUT THE AUTHOR

*Colleen Williams-Thompson
A Woman With A Purpose*

I was born in Trinidad and Tobago. I moved to Boston in 1983. Despite every negative situation I have been though, I am good, I am over it. I love to write and travel. My favorite place is Barbados, I love to go over there and find myself. I stay in a little villa by myself and walk to the beach and chill, I have my moments with the water. I just watch the waves; that is my healing.

After many failed relationships, I had to find myself. I had to pull back and see what I was doing wrong; after some serious searching, it was not me. I am still the same kind, loving person. My favorite number is three, so I said after three failed relationships, they all can't be that bad, so I went out and tried again. I was amazed how this one started out. Although I went in with a positive attitude, I still had my guard up just in case. I was hoping this one would be the last one. With a string of toxic relationships dating right back to my son's father, I deserve some kind of happiness. In no time he showed his true colors. He finally admitted that he wasn't ready for a relationship but he wanted to continue dating me. I told him I date with a purpose. I don't have trial periods where I date a lot of men, I date with potential. I am looking for someone serious.

    Truth be told, I didn't even like myself very much. I made a promise to myself that I need to pull back and love myself more. The energy and love that I was giving to the world, I had to give that to myself. I was treating people the way I wanted them to treat me, but when I started treating myself the way I want to be treated I saw a complete turnaround. If I was looking for my king, I had to treat myself like a queen. I no longer felt "worthless and good for nothing" since that is all I heard so that stayed in my mind. I was always being used and taken advantage of. I had to stop pleasing people and started to please myself.

    I made up my mind for the first time in my entire life I had to put myself first; if no one was going to fight for me I had to fight for myself. At the end of the day no one is going to love me the way I can. I also realized that no matter what happened in my life it is in the past. I can't look back, I can't do anything about it. I'm not going to keep taking the blame for someone else's mistake.

Being single and doing my soul-searching gave me the chance to connect with a lot of women who were hurting and who were experiencing the same pain with relationship issues and abuse. A lot of women want that security blanket, but like me, I was looking in the wrong direction. I started speaking to more and more women, while I was teaching them, I was healing and learning. I wanted to fix myself. I didn't want to be broken and bitter anymore. I wanted to be that beautiful strong woman I know I could be.

I didn't want to end up with a broken man and I know a man did not want to deal with a broken woman. So, I had to be a better woman.

I am not even looking; 'they say the good ones sneak up on you when you are not looking.' So, I guess I'll wait till that happens. In the meantime, I will continue loving myself. I know there is true love after hurting, it just takes time.

In my second book "Stop," I speak to and for women who have been Sexually Abused or had to deal with Domestic Violence while being married to an unfaithful husband. Teaching men and women how to take all negative situations and make it positive and empowering them to do better and be better. In the end we can all learn to forgive and heal. Moving forward from Bitter and Broken to Beautiful and Blessed. Dear victims of any kind of abuse: If you have been touched, sexually abused, or in any Domestic violence situation please reach out and get help.

First thing you need to stop doing is listening to everyone else who never went through what you went through. We all want to heal and wish it never happened, but let's face it, it did. Some people can be so rude, malicious, disrespectful and just plain ignorant, you have been through enough so don't let them knock you off your pedestal. Stop thinking one day when you wake up it will miraculously be gone: it's not happening. No one said it will be easy, but together we can get through it.

Enough of barricading yourself and trying really hard to act like it didn't happen, because as we all know it did and knowing is half the battle. Now that we have acknowledged that let's move on to healing.

I know you want to wave a magic wand and your higher power will come and magically fix everything. Trust me, you will never be the same person you were, it will be on your mind, but you can heal from it.

Personally, it took 30 years for me to get help; I don't suggest that for anyone. Get help right away. I don't want you or anyone else to wait that long.

I grew up in Trinidad, so my country did not have all the resources the American system has. Whatever happened just happened; we had to deal with it. At the end of the day, just know it wasn't your fault. You didn't abuse yourself, you didn't hurt yourself. Don't continue to blame yourself or beat up yourself; instead use that time to give yourself that unconditional love that you deserve.

Take this pledge with me: Forgive your past, release the old pain and give yourself permission to begin new with a clean slate! I'm ready to move on.

My pain became my praise. My fight made me famous.

My story was my glory. My tears covered my fears.

My wounds became my wisdom.

Colleen Williams Thompson
Boston Mass
Bridgeport Connecticut

www.ingramcontent.com/pod-product-compliance
Lightning Source LLC
Chambersburg PA
CBHW071422080526
44587CB00014B/1719